SACRED PAVEMENT

A do-it-yourself guide to spirituality in the city

BY ERIN CLARK

SACRED PAVEMENT:

A DO-IT-YOURSELF GUIDE TO SPIRITUALITY IN THE CITY

The book information is catalogued as follows;
Author Name(s): Erin Clark
Title: Sacred Pavement: A do-it-yourself guide to spirituality in the city

Description; First Edition
1st Edition, 2021
Book Design & Typesetting by Michael Maloney

ISBN 978-1-913479-85-5 (paperback)

ISBN 978-1-913479-86-2 (ebook)

Published by That Guy's House
www.ThatGuysHouse.com

COMMENDATIONS
FOR SACRED PAVEMENT

Sacred Pavement is a necessary and needed road map for finding wonder and spiritual connection in the city. Erin Clark skillfully encourages urban dwellers to slow down amidst fast paced lives in hurried environments to find their souls without needing to escape to the country. She does this with such humour, love and enthusiasm that we may just find more and more people escaping to the city instead. Put on your walking shoes and embark on an everyday sacred pilgrimage right to your own backyard. There is beauty to be found in the most unexpected places.

— *Vanessa Sage, PhD*

'Sacred Pavement' is a treat, just like a walk in my beloved neighbourhood in the good company of Erin herself pondering what matters in life. Erin's encouragement to undertake an urban adventure for the sake of our soul is both urgent and playful as she shares stories and tips to help us create our own maps of belonging. As you hold this book in your hands, look down at your feet and give thanks for them, because they are about to take you and your senses on a spiritual journey through in-between places to new vistas and back to yourself again. Her practical wisdom guides us to find our own holy moments in the city, but take heed, as we learn to re-inhabit our everyday places as sacred spaces, the wonder and walking is now ours to undertake - enjoy!

— *Kate Monkhouse, Executive Officer, Creators of Peace*

With the eyes of an American living in London, Erin shares her perceptions of various aspects concerning life in a modern, bustling city. Looking beneath the surface with the eye of the heart, she shares insights and offers practical exercises to help the reader reflect on a variety of encounters described in the chapter. Without expecting the reader to identify with any particular spirituality or religion...she invites the reader to stop and look at what can easily be taken for granted in order to find deeper delight in our environment.

— *Fr. John-Francis Friendship*

CONTENTS

FOREWORD

In the first few months after becoming Bishop of Stepney in the Church of England – an area which covers Tower Hamlets, Hackney, and Islington – my daughter and I joined a sponsored night walk led by Beyond the Streets, an organization which supports women who are caught up in prostitution. As we walked through the streets of Whitechapel and along the Thames path, we learned about those who have been sexually exploited in the capital and those still facing exploitation today. We also remembered by name some of those who have been victims of violence – including Mary Ann Nichols, Annie Chapman, Elizabeth Stride, Catherine Eddowes and Mary Jane Kelly, all victims of the murderer known as Jack the Ripper.

Part way along the route, we bumped up against one of the commercial walking tours which seems to glorify Jack the Ripper's brutal past, as it takes tourists through some key sites of the capital's most infamous murder mystery. On the tour, the murdered women are barely mentioned and are not named. A conversation followed, evidently to the annoyance of the group's Ripper guide, initiated by some members of his group, and we explained why we were praying at a memorial wall of ribbons, on the fence of Southwark's Crossbones Graveyard, to victims of violence and "the outcast dead." We reflected together on how remembering each victim by name might be a more worthy task than venerating, for profit, the murderous Jack.

The prophet Jeremiah tells us "to seek the welfare of the city where I have sent you into exile, and pray to the LORD on its behalf, for in its welfare you will find your welfare." I have always loved city walking, finding it thought-provoking, stirring, energizing. Now it is part of my daily discipline of prayer, whether ambling along the school run and contemplating the day ahead, dashing for the tube sending up swift prayers for people and situations, or stomping round the park, chewing over a difficult issue or relationship, in each case asking God to disentangle and redeem the intricate complexities of life and ministry and set me on the right path. It is solved by walking. It is solved, and we are saved, as we walk with God.

Walking that night in solidarity with the victims of violence, I became acutely conscious of my task to pray for this part of the city of London. Memorial by memorial, I needed to understand its past. Landmark by landmark, like a cartographer poring over battlements and borders, I needed to interrogate its power. Sleeping bag by sleeping bag, their belongings swept away into dumpsters, I needed to notice those whose bed is the pavement. Name by name, I needed to pray for all its citizens, and especially those in need today. Footstep by footstep, I needed, through my prayers, to walk with all those who are seeking to shape this incredible city for the future, so that my daughter's generation might, in appreciating its past, and loving its present, live prayerfully into its future with its welfare on their hearts.

In *Sacred Pavement*, Mother Erin brings alive the circularity of praying for a city and being formed by it in prayer. The Danish architect and urban planner Jan Gehl once said, "What you count, you care for."[1] People of prayer know that what you pray about, you care for – and also that what you care about shapes how you pray. As we seek the welfare of the city, the city teaches us more deeply what welfare, wellbeing and good dwelling in God together can look like. It helps us to move beyond the idolatry and selfishness which mar community life, and to find the words to cry to God for justice, for the needs of the foreigner, the fatherless, and the widow, and for a safe and just home for all.

With the curious eyes of an urban planner, a map maker, a charity shop rummager, a commuter, a neighbour,and with the heart of a priest, Mother Erin reminds us that we don't need to find sanctuary from the city in order to pray for it and for all God's creation, but that if we will pause, slow our footsteps, notice and attend to our surroundings, the city will provide all that we need to journey well with God. What follows is not only our own refreshment and renewal, though we may notice both, it is also the sharpening of our prophetic voice, equipping us better for challenge and change. What follows is the entwining of our lives, through prayer paced out on the city's pavements with the will of God.

Walk prayerfully. Speak prophetically. Live intentionally. Ask God through you to shape the city in what you name, celebrate, resist, and cherish. Ask God to give you courage for the journey as you advocate for the foreigner, the fatherless, the widow, and all who have not yet found a safe home.

Seek the welfare of the city and know that in it you will find your welfare.

— The Rt Revd Dr Joanne Grenfell, Bishop of Stepney

[1] ULI Europe's Real Estate Forum in Copenhagen in June 2019: Creating and Sustaining Flexible Spaces: https://urbanland.uli.org/planning-design/architect-jan-gehls-philosophy-on-future-proofing-old-cities/.

CHAPTER 0

First things first

The spirituality stock photo problem

You know the photos I'm talking about. Perhaps they are on social media. You might spot them on a greeting card or on the cover of a book, a spread in a magazine or newspaper — probably one of those frivolous sections only published at the weekend. There is sun, usually, and some form of foliage. Palm trees seem to be best, but a carpet of mountain evergreens will do. Against the background of a View with a capital V, you see some blissed-out person or people, tiny when compared to the stunning natural vista surrounding them. If they don't have their back to you, they're making the sort of contented face you're sure you never quite achieve during meditation. Maybe they are doing yoga on a deserted dock next to a picture perfect log cabin. Maybe they have just scaled Mount Kilimanjaro and are beatific. Whatever is going on, they are at one with their stunning natural surroundings. Lucky them.

Even if this image isn't intended directly to sell you something, you may find yourself longing for the same idle moment you see pictured in front of you: cocooned by the beach or the mountains or the wooded path, breathing the pure air, slowing down to the pace set by this corner of the earth. You begin longing to be comfortably marooned in some true wilderness where the impressive scale, colour and drama of the environment pulls you out of your daily worries and undertakings and helps you know that you are small when compared to this and to take comfort in that smallness.

This feeling isn't the same kind you get standing beside a sixty-storey glass building, surrounded by miles of tarmac and streets on a grid. That's a different thing altogether, isn't it? It's not usually an uncomplicated moment of wonder or soaking in straightforward beauty. On that city street there's likely pressure instead of relaxation and noise where there might be silence. Though you might feel small looking up at the glass infinity of a skyscraper, it's not comforting but daunting.

What is it that makes these images so different — one awe-inspiring, deeply stirring to the spirit, and the other a literal pain in the neck? The answer lies in what *spirituality* has come to mean in much of western culture. If you're reading this book you almost certainly have your own working definition of what spirituality is, or at least what your own spirituality looks like. My working definition is this: spirituality is returning to a sense of connection with the transcendent, of perceiving the bigger picture of this earth and beyond, of perceiving beauty and mystery which is bigger than yourself but to which you have some kind of access.

Connection with the transcendent does not equal escaping from the immanent, however. It means returning to this sense of connection within the everyday moments of our lives. Spirituality is a practice which can inform every dimension of our lives, and it cannot be reduced simply to our thoughts, feelings or our participation in community life.The life of the spirit has to do with the centre of who we are: beings with the spark of eternity at our core, a spark which calls out to that which is eternal and transcendent everywhere (and within everyone) else.

Currently in much of western culture, the notion of transcendence is much easier to represent with stock photos of escape, of gorgeous vistas and conventionally 'ideal' bodies, than in the messy realities of life, especially urban life. Where then does that leave the 55% of the world's population who live in urban areas? For city-dwellers, it can be easy to fall into the trap of seeing spirituality as some form of escape from the grind of daily life in our cities. This is the trap of finding our spiritual lives full of phrases that begin with the words, *If only...*

If only I could get out of the city to go on more retreats or holidays.

If only my neighbours weren't so loud, I could pray more easily.

If only life wasn't so expensive, I could go to more yoga classes.

If only I didn't have to commute, I could have so much time for journaling as part of my spiritual practice.

If only I felt more connected to those around me.

If only my city weren't so ugly, I'd feel more connected to beauty.

If only my city were a more peaceful or safe place to live.

How can urban dwellers escape the 'If only...' trap? We do this by shifting the ways we allow ourselves to live out our spiritualities.

From the sticks to the skyscrapers

When I was twenty-one years old I relocated from a rural township in the United States — where the nearest 'town', 10 miles away, had a population of 950 — to London in the United Kingdom: one of the world's biggest, messiest and most complex cities. To say there was a bit of culture shock was an understatement. I had lived in London twice briefly as a student, first in a fairly leafy northern part of the city where the loudest noises were the Wednesday night crowds passing my street en route from the Underground station to the Arsenal stadium. Next, though, I spent time in Tower Hamlets, a deceptively rural sounding inner-city borough known for its high rates of crime, social deprivation, large immigrant population, ineffective local government and what the newspapers referred to euphemistically as 'grit and grime'.

Spoiler alert: it's not really a euphemism.

I came back to London because of a love affair: not with a human Londoner but with the city itself. Most of my family and friends were convinced I must have a secret lover overseas somewhere — because why else would I up sticks so dramatically? If I had to move to a city, couldn't I pick a nice American one? As the cliché goes, though, the heart wants what it wants, and I followed what my heart wanted: London. Acclimatising to London meant realising that the pressures of everyday life were completely different to rural life. Sure, I didn't have to shovel snow off my car for at least three months of the year and worry about pipes freezing; but it wasn't long before I noticed rising house prices, low air quality and sundry other issues were pushing people out of the city constantly. Though the density of the city's population overall was increasing, I met more and more people (and not just those who were middle class or white) who were starting a family, trying to buy a house, longing for more simplicity, or simply searching for their version of 'the good life' — and they all seemed to hanker after leaving London altogether.

One such acquaintance of mine, in the throes of this hankering, compared city-dwelling to being stuck in an abusive relationship. When she said this I was brought up short, recalling how painfully strong my own love had been for London at first. It had made me think I could be brave enough to make this move, to believe there were places for me to belong here. Always a person with a deep, if occasionally doubtful, spirituality, I had arrived here without taking any thought for how my own spiritual life was shaped by the rural places where I had grown up and gone to study. I hadn't realised that moving here would require a complete recalibration of my spiritual senses. If I was going to relate to London as anything other than an abusive partner, if I was going to go from living my spirituality not in spite of my city but in cooperation with her, I was going to have to adjust. Significantly. I was going to have to discover spiritual senses I never knew I had.

Like so many other city dwellers, during this time I took great pleasure in London's parks and fled regularly to the countryside to walk up and down one hill or another. On my walls were photos of beautiful getaways, taken myself or ripped from travel magazines. At some point, however, even this pattern began to be exhausting. 'I just need to get out of the city to recharge my batteries,' I'd find myself saying. Or, 'I survive by going running in Victoria Park because at least it's green there.' I would go on retreats to monasteries buried in the countryside and take walking holidays to the European continent. The language of my spirituality, and what's more, the practice of it, was constantly shaped around getting away from the city.

I began to notice the images I was drawn to in newspapers, books and social media. They were what I jokingly called the 'spirituality stock photos' above: sundrenched, at-one-with-nature, tantalisingly distant ideals. Something in me grew grumpy, then resentful, then downright angry that my spiritual life, and the spiritual lives of billions of other people, would have to be reduced to this advertisement-fuelled escapism. It wasn't that I didn't find my city loud, frustrating, occasionally dirty and completely confounding; it was that I didn't want the whole of my spiritual life to be spent running away.

Fast forward over a decade, and I'm still here in London. I've shuttled back and forth across the ocean and lived outside 'the Big Smoke' for a few years. It has been long enough to see streets I once knew well become unrecognisable, long enough to start using *UK English* autocorrect on my computer, long enough to put 'Londoner' in my bios. Long enough to fall in and out of love with this place over and over again, to find and hone some new spiritual senses.

The notion of 'spiritual senses' is a contested one. I use the phrase to mean particular qualities, and practices drawn from those qualities, which make it easier for a person to live out their spirituality. Throughout the book, you might spot the following spiritual senses at work in my essays and in the work you're encouraged to do. I go into more depth on some than others, and no doubt you may find yourself reflecting on some which are not on this list:

- Awareness / Attention
- Wonder
- Playfulness / Humour
- Discomfort
- Curiosity
- Discipline / Commitment
- Imagination
- Stillness
- Empathy
- Sensuality
- Humility
- Reflection
- Mapmaking (I'll return to that in the next section)

Spiritual senses are meant to be used *where we are*, rather than in some kind of imagined ideal escape of the stock photos. I have written this book as a challenge and encouragement to those who feel forced towards this escapism, to those who find themselves stuck in a spiral of spiritual 'if only'. A spirituality of escape is no way to live. It is the opposite of being present to each holy moment. It is possible — even fun and life-giving — to learn to cooperate with the urban environment in the pursuit of an authentic spiritual life. This book is a guide to that pursuit.

It's your pursuit, though; not mine. You may be reading this from the United Kingdom, the USA, or neither. I mention several different cities which have left a mark on me over the years, and my intention is that you can relate to the themes of this book no matter where you are or what size of city you inhabit. My role in all this is to be your accompanist whilst you figure out your own solo.

Mapmaking: what you'll be doing in this book

Just above, I listed 'mapmaking' as a spiritual sense. This might strike you as odd, but hear me out. This book is an invitation to urban exploration for the sake of your soul. It is meant to be accessible and practical: along with things to read, there will be things to observe and to do. You can choose to work on these tasks alone or with a friend. At the end of the book, there is a chapter on how you might use this book with groups, or share what you have discovered throughout the course of reading and exploring. A word of caution, especially if you are very extroverted, a 'people person', or if your daily roles or jobs consist largely in serving others: be careful to safeguard some time for solitary reflection and exploration. It can be so easy to outsource the development of our own spirituality to others, and to tell ourselves that we don't have time to focus on our own journeys.

Conversely, if you are finding it all too easy to do the work in this book by yourself, dare to invite a friend to be part of one or two of the tasks early on. Another pair of eyes is a valuable asset so that we don't get stuck in our own spiritual feedback loops.

Each chapter of this book hones in on a different aspect of urban life, weaving together personal stories with reflections on how that aspect of life can become truly part of one's spiritual life. Each chapter finishes with some practical tasks. I've framed these tasks and the reflection they're meant to inspire as Urban Adventures, and you'll find that many of them involve going beyond journal prompts to sketching or illustrating, making maps and drawings.

My fascination with maps runs deep: I am intrigued by the unlimited number of ways there are to represent space and place, sight and sound, hope and fear and memory on a two dimensional piece of paper or a screen. Maps are a wonderfully flexible way to help you document your urban explorations. The best thing is that you absolutely do not need to be a great artist to make them. Mine are full of stick figures and scribbled-out first tries; almost everything in them is not to any kind of scale. Skill in drawing is not the point. The point is beginning to think more spatially, by which I mean thinking of your physical environment, the urban space around you, as *spiritual space*. This is why I see mapmaking as a spiritual sense — because of how it reframes space spirituality, to help rather than hinder spiritual growth. Urban space becomes somewhere you don't always need to flee in order to be free.

In this book I will be encouraging you to make loads of different maps: many of the practical tasks come with a 'map this' or 'try making a map in this way'. To give you as much space as possible, I encourage you to buy a plain journal in which to do this work, rather than including blank pages in this book. If you find it easier to keep your map very basic and then use that map as a collection of journal prompts, try that approach. But don't limit yourself to journaling or writing only. After all, a really interesting, juicy map is one with plenty of writing in it: road names, keys, landmarks, even the occasional *Here be Dragons.*

Packing List

- This book
- A journal (at least a5 size; preferably plain or with dots, rather than lines)
- A good pen
- Weather-worthy shoes and clothes
- Water
- Snacks

Where we're *not* going in this book

Before starting out on any journey, it's wise to get a sense of where the journey might or might not take you. First off, this book won't take you deep into an academic consideration of the urban environment. Though there are some great academic texts out there on urban spaces, this book's aim is practical, not theoretical. You can always follow up some of the books, films or other resources to which I refer, but try not to let that going-down-the-rabbit-hole get in the way of actually getting out on your Urban Adventures.

Another thing this book is not is a guide to mindful living. Mindful attention to the present moment is an obviously useful spiritual practice - a spiritual sense which will be helpful for you. In my experience, however, the word *mindfulness* can often be used as a means of silencing conversation around spirituality, for fear of conflict, confusion or pushy proselytisation between people of different religious or spiritual traditions. This book is written from a place of gratitude for the varied spiritual or faith traditions of this world, with a deep and humble desire to begin conversations between people of different traditions. City dwellers are bound to rub up against people who don't share their specific beliefs. I believe that is a positive thing, in fact, one of the most fascinating things about city living. This book is meant to encourage you to be curious about the diversity of spiritual paths around you, not to simply practise mindfulness as a lowest common denominator.

This book does not promise to Revolutionise Your Spiritual Life in 10 Easy Steps. Even if you put 110% into the Urban Adventures, you will probably get to the end of it and find you have so much more to explore and so many more ways your city has become more mysterious to you. A revolution in your spiritual life may well have begun, but it won't be finished. Ultimately, this book is about slowing down not speeding up the 'revolutions' or turnings-around in our urban, spiritual lives. The themes in this book will hopefully be ones that you can continue exploring, in whatever way makes sense for you, for all the years you make a city your home.

Finally, although this book is about practicing spirituality in urban environments, I'm certainly not trying to say that the natural world is bad nor that spending time in rural areas isn't an absolutely worthwhile way to nurture your spirit. On the contrary, I have written a whole chapter entitled 'Finding Stubborn Nature' addressing exactly this topic. I'd encourage you to listen deeply to what you need in terms of spending time outside your city, because rural contexts can be immensely healing and nourishing to the soul. This book's focus, as I've said above, is to help you find nourishment not only in the rural or the natural but within (and not in spite of) the city.

Housekeeping

There are two points of quick housekeeping to do before we start. The first is a note about safety. Although this book is exploratory, aimed at developing curiosity and courage, it is worth reminding you to do all your exploring with due regard for your personal safety. When we open ourselves up to spiritual exploration we are becoming more deliberately vulnerable, so it's important to make sure we take a moment to consider safety, alongside the risk. This could be as simple as watching where you're going. As you let yourself enjoy noticing new parts of a city, don't forget to mind the kerbs, bicycle crossings and so on. Safety is also about trusting your gut when going places you have never been before or perhaps, taking a friend along with you on some explorations. If you find it hard to differentiate between apprehension about trying new things and places and trusting your gut, or if you notice that you frequently choose not to do things because of your worries about safety, check these fears and talk over your plans with a trusted person who can help you figure out which is which. Sometimes it is wise — it is enough — to write 'Here be dragons' or 'Here I knew not to go further' on your map.

The second piece of housekeeping is about the language that I use in this book. You'll notice that I vary my word choices, mentioning words like Spirit, God, the Divine, spirituality, faith, the self, the inner life, in the context of the human spiritual journey. For some of you, the word God/Goddess/Goddex may describe the object of your spirituality and devotion. Others will use the words Spirit or Universe, and still others may think of the Higher Self or *psyche* (that word which helps give us the idea of a soul). This book is meant to give you space to use the language you're used to and also to try another language on for size. I hope that what I offer here is helpful, no matter the angle from which you approach your spiritual journey.

My own angle on spirituality is from within what Ian Adams calls the 'ancient and unfolding Jesus tradition' — that is, Christianity. I'm an Anglican priest and that social location and confessional posture undeniably informs what I write and gives me a working spirituality which is grounded in a sense of wonder. (There's one of those spiritual senses!) I see spirituality as an activity, cultivating senses and practices which make me more able to perceive the presence of the Divine within and beyond the fabric of this beautiful world. Throughout this book I will keep drawing us back to that sense of awe or wonder.

At some points in this book, you may find yourself asking: 'Wait a second, what does this have to do with spirituality?'

Architecture, politics, travel, history, neighbourliness: these might seem to have little to do with our individual spiritual practices. I come from a tradition within Christianity, however, that has preserved strong warnings against quickly or easily separating the 'sacred' versus the 'secular', the 'holy' versus the 'profane'. To my mind the real spiritual revolution in the life of any individual or community is the one that follows the question: 'What if *all of life* were sacred, and all our actions within life inherently spiritual because of that?' If all our lives are sacred, then no longer can we put some aspects of life in a 'secular' category (doing the washing up, chatting to a neighbour, answering emails, reading about some local history, unpacking from a trip). Instead, we find ways of leaning into grace even and especially in those areas which seem least overtly spiritual.

You certainly don't have to share that exact definition of spirituality or the sacred, or be a Christian, or have any interest in Christianity or organised religion to read and use this book, though! I've written with deliberate openness to different approaches to spirituality and faith, precisely because, as I mentioned above, living out your spirituality in the city means regular contact with people whose paths are different to yours. If you come up against language which is unfamiliar or difficult to you in this book, please feel free to substitute language which works. Or, if you like, you may choose to journal or meditate on which words or phrases stirred up questions for you.

Whistle-stop tour

In short, this book walks readers through different aspects of urban life and encourages deeper exploration of them. We begin in Chapter 1 with the topic of *Walking the walk* — the basic practice of slowing down your urban experience to just the pace of one step after another. In chapter 2, we look up: *Reading architecture* and relating to the built environment. Chapter 3 on *Commuting* follows, for those many of us who have journeys to and from work or other commitments. We spend Chapter 4 on the topic of urban *Thrift and abundance* — reconsidering our attitudes towards money and resources as urban dwellers.

We can't be city people without plenty of neighbours so we take a look at *Neighbourliness* next in Chapter 5, and how our neighbours influence our spiritual lives. Our current neighbours aren't the only ones whose lives have a bearing on ours, though, so Chapter 6, *Neighbours in time*, will introduce us to ways of being spiritually curious to the history of our city and those who have lived there before.

All cities, no matter how straightforward, have mysterious or hidden sides to them and *Seeking the hidden* is what we'll be doing in Chapter 7. In Chapter 8 we come back to the natural world with *Finding stubborn nature* — reminding ourselves that the boundaries between 'urban' and 'rural' are rarely as clear-cut as we might like to think.

Chapter 9 takes a look at how we approach travel to and from our cities, as most of us will be travelling *There and back again* at various times for work, holidays or other reasons. And, for those of us who have left a city or cities permanently, Chapter 10 explores the spirituality of *Taking your leave* and doing so well.

By the end of this book, you will have had the opportunity to reframe all these facets of your urban life in ways which, I hope, will help you see them and participate them as helps to your spirituality, rather than hindrances. You'll have a map, hand-drawn by you, to help you escape the escapism and to spot the sacred in every ordinary pavement. Good luck and *bon voyage!*

Setting out: before Urban Adventuring

Crack open that new journal and give yourself the gift of a bit of time in reflection, using the following prompts:

Write about the times which you've spent living in cities, listing the adjectives that come to mind to describe each of those places, maybe 5 or 10 words apiece. Draw a timeline of your life and try to figure out how much of it has been spent as an urban dweller. What about your city is most obstructive to the spiritual life you would like to inhabit? What is most helpful?

Think also about the adjectives you use to describe yourself, and what you were like when you lived in or experienced those cities. Were you frugal? Busy? Successful? Lonely? Productive? Just figuring yourself out? Using a pie chart for each city, divide it up into slices to represent those adjectives.

What images of spiritual fulfilment (those 'spiritual stock photos') can you bring to mind and can you sketch them? Do you notice any common themes between them? Have those experiences of peace and fulfilment ever been yours? Where?

Finally, it's important when setting off a journey to have a thought about destination. As all good pilgrims will tell you, the destination is rarely as important as the journey itself, however, the intentions which underlie the destination give shape to how we make it, with all its twists and turns. So, where do you want this book to take you?

CHAPTER 1

Walking the walk

The battle of the blisters

Blisters really are the worst, aren't they? I am a person whose genetics dictated from the start that I would have large feet: I wear men's shoes, mostly, or spring for expensive ones from a shop endearingly named 'Long Tall Sally'. I have a memory of what my grandfather used to say when I complained that I'd worn out yet another pair of shoes at the tip, a common occurrence my mother would call 'having hungry toes'. Not to be outdone by mom's attempt at wit, my grandfather would joke, 'You know, Erin, you'd be a lot taller if you didn't have so much turned under.' As if I didn't know that already, Grandpa.

Being large of foot comes with its advantages: being tall and able to reach more things, and also regularly to get mistaken for a man, causing mortification for my mis-genderers and hilarity for me. The main and rather boring disadvantage is difficulty in finding shoes, manifested for me in something I came to call the Battle of the Blisters. For me this battle only really began after I moved to London and began to learn what it meant to live a walking life.

It's not that I never walked long distances before moving to a city, but those were always *purposeful* events: going hiking in the state park, a day spent chasing down antiques in a chocolate-box town, a Saturday morning doing yard work. Those activities were easy to find shoes for: broken-in boots and scruffy, sturdy sneakers. When I lived in the country there wasn't much need for covering distances on foot. Driving or ambling between locations for work or study meant my everyday shoes never felt too much wear and tear. Then the city happened.

TL;DR: ballet flats hold up for approximately 2 minutes in a British springtime, and then they don't anymore.

As most American tourists will tell you, walking European cities is A LOT when you're not used to it. The same is true for North American cities; those extra fifteen minutes here, twenty minutes there constitute a sneaky bit of exercise as well as wreaking havoc on your shoes. The same goes for your feet, if your shoes don't fit quite right.

2010 was the turning point of the Battle of the Blisters for me. Not once, not twice, but *three* times that year I managed to develop terrible blisters on my feet from the wrong shoes. Each time I did a terrific job of feeling sorry for myself for my poor choices in footwear and my too-long walks. Like some kind of fairytale, I suppose, I had to learn a lesson by having a few failures first.

That year, I traveled to the USA to visit my parents for Christmas. On the couch and full of Christmas dinner leftovers, surrounded by that familiar joy and tension of being a temporary, grown-up visitor in my childhood home, I was longing for a good long walk but with a blizzard outside, that wasn't going to be possible for a while. It wasn't just a walk I wanted, though, but also what walking had become for me: space to breathe and pray.

Suddenly it struck me just how regular and spiritually grounding my practice of walking had become. Of course in London I walk out of necessity often, to get from one place to another. But I realised it was no longer odd for me to set out on a walk to clear my mind, have a pray, or turn over a problem in my head until it began to unravel. In a way that had never happened for me in the country — where walks were taken in order to see something, visit a space, or to Do Some Exercise — walking had become an instinctive spiritual practice for me, one enabled by my city's geography. My repeated blister episodes were simply part of becoming a city walker; it was taking my shoe-buying habits a minute to catch up with my spiritual habits!

In that moment, I was able to reframe the Battle of the Blisters as one I needed to lose in order to realise how great a grace I'd found in walking as a spiritual practice. Walking had become a costly but necessary means of caring for my soul. Often, perhaps, we think of self- or soul-care and as some nice treat we can just pour liberally on top of a pile of unpleasant things to make them a bit easier to manage. Feeling disconnected spiritually? Go buy yourself something. I am as guilty as anyone for falling into this trap.

In truth, however, caring for the state of your soul isn't just a spoonful of sugar that makes it possible to persevere through hard things. It is a commitment, one which will reshape and recondition the whole of our lives. Practices like walking are more than just nice occasional treats: they are the means by which our spirituality exists at all. Walking as a spiritual practice had changed my attitudes to time, transport and prayer. So long as I was going to engage with this practice, I realised on that wintry afternoon, my urban life was calling me to invest in some more durable shoes.

Solvitur ambulando

City dwellers walk for numerous reasons, most of them having little to do with spirituality. Sometimes walking is just walking, and we pay little attention to its spiritual dimension. Like me, many people accidentally discover walking as a spiritual practice because walking for some length is part of everyday life. In my experience, urban spirituality often develops in this way: by necessity. By reflecting on the patterns that already make up our lives, we begin to realise how rich those patterns are.

At some point after that Christmastime realisation of how important walking had become to my inner life, the phrase *solvitur ambulando* found me. I wish I could remember where I read it first but, as is the way with wisdom passed down through generations, the important thing was that I learnt it, not when or where. Attributed in its original form to ancient Greek philosopher Diogenes, this phrase translates: 'it is solved by walking'. Legend has it that Diogenes was fed up with his fellow philosophers and their endless rhetorical arguments — on one particular day, the topic of discussion was, 'Is motion real?' A grumpy Diogenes decided he'd had enough of philosophical proofs. He got up from the conversation and walked away, shouting over his shoulder, 'It is solved by walking'. Motion was real; he was moving. A mic drop moment in the ancient world.

On the one hand, then, *solvitur ambulando* is a mantra for keeping us grounded in our physical realities. For those of us on spiritual journeys there's a perpetual temptation to spend a lot of time inside in our thoughts and emotional centres, processing and wondering and thinking all the thoughts, feeling all the feels. In one sense *solvitur ambulando* says, 'Want to know what's real? Use your senses. Get up and walk.' Remember: there is ground beneath your feet. Start there. If you're an urban dweller — that ground is urban ground.

It's not just about physical groundedness, though. Our spiritual lives are as real as the ground beneath our feet, if harder to talk about sometimes because we have lost confidence in talking about our spiritual senses and experiences with the same regularity as our physical, common senses and experiences. *Solvitur ambulando* insists that these two need not be separate nor one ranked as more important than the other. Just as motion is its own proof, the enacted spiritual life is its own proof. Spirituality is nothing if not practical, and practicable. Put another way: whatever 'it' is that needs solving in your life, the answer will probably not lie in lying still.

You might read this and think *solvitur ambulando* is just a fancy way of saying, 'So you've got a problem? Walk it off!' However, the phrase goes far deeper than that. 'Walk it off!' seems to treat walking (physical activity) as a means to an end (mental or spiritual clarity). It's a pretty mechanical way of looking at ourselves, as if we are robots that just need to be fed certain things to produce certain results.

A spirituality of walking is not primarily about getting results — though the benefits of walking are many — but about being open to whatever the walk brings. Walking can become a truly spiritual practice only when we realise that because we bother to set out, anything is possible. What began and might end as simply a walk to burn off some energy after a stressful meeting might end up being no more than that. Or, we might be guided to an understanding of why it was so stressful or what dynamics may have been at play, or to some other unrelated insight.

The biggest joy of walking as a spiritual practice, for me, is precisely its reliable unpredictability. I cherish the way that the roads and routes that are so familiar can open up their secrets — and our own — to us again and again. No matter how weak our wills or vague our intentions, just getting out for a walk seems to bring strength and clarity where I need it. So start out on the walk — even if you're not feeling prayerful, even if paying attention or being mindful is too much. Sometimes a walk is just a walk; sometimes it is the beginning of something else.

Approaches

Walking as a spiritual practice is an enormous topic, and one on which most of the world's spiritual traditions have centuries of wisdom to share. I'd like to look at just two different ways of approaching urban walking: psychogeography and pilgrimage.

Psychogeography

If you've never heard the word psychogeography, don't worry! It's not as impenetrable as it sounds. Popularised by writers and artists making work in response to their ever-changing urban contexts, psychogeography brings together the 'psyche' (a word which we often think means *mind* but is closer in origin to how we might understand the word *soul*) and 'geography' or the study of places. You might say that psychogeography is the exploration of the 'soul of a place'. For that reason, it's one great way to approach a spirituality of walking — especially urban walking.

Whether or not places have such a thing as a soul or some kind of eternal dimension is something which is conceptualised very differently depending on what religious or philosophical traditions you come from. You don't have to be a fully signed-up believer in Gaia, however, to observe and appreciate that places are more complex, more layered, than just what meets the eye. By virtue of their history, places act as a container for the joys, struggles, sufferings and celebrations of the past. This is why people travel to visit former battlefields, ancient temples or centuries-old marketplaces: to hear with their spiritual ears these echoes of purpose. In any given street corner in a city you might be standing on a spot that has seen a market, a temple and/or a battle of some kind. The history in a city can be incredibly dense and the clues to discovering that history can be well-hidden. Patience and playfulness are required.

A psychogeographical approach to urban walking offers us two key insights. The first is exactly this sense of playfulness or meandering, of not following our predetermined routes too quickly or automatically. This sort of wandering involves a willingness to be distracted or drawn off course and to recognise that distractions might be of Spirit. If spirituality is about seeking moments of wonder, then those moments will be hard to find if every step, landmark and turn in the walk is planned out beforehand.

The second insight of psychogeography is the importance of documenting your walks in some way. While we humans are amazing in how much our brains can hold, there are limits. Plus, we might get a very different impression of the soul of a place from one visit to another. Keeping a record of your walks, and not being afraid to be creative, goofy and free in how you do so, is doing a bit of psychogeography. You are acting as a witness to your own spiritual history, lived out in walking these urban spaces.

You might be thinking, 'But how do I know whether I'm *really* tuning into the soul of this place? What if I miss those clues? Isn't this all totally subjective? I could think of a place as super joyful when I'm in a good mood, or depressing if I'm feeling a bit grim.' The answer is of course city walking is subjective. Of course your mood will affect how you go about it. There is always a risk that we only see what we want to see. But it's important to remember the soul of a place is not a static thing, it will always be in dialogue with those who bring their spiritual attention to it. What's more, we can learn to listen more closely by walking these spiritual paths (both literally and metaphorically) with others, and by returning to the same urban spaces in our walks.

Pilgrimage

If psychogeography helps us as urban walkers to consider *how* we walk and *how* we record our walks, pilgrimage asks us *why* we walk. Pilgrimages are by definition purposeful journeys, focused on a destination and a reason for getting there. Usually made over a number of days or weeks to a particularly special or holy site, pilgrimages traditionally are made in the company of other people, often strangers. They are traditionally, but not always, made at least partially on foot. Europe alone has thousands of pilgrimage routes criss-crossing it in a sacred web.

Many of the world's major faiths encourage the practice of pilgrimage: Tibetan Buddhists making arduous kora, devout Muslims thronging to holy sites such as Mecca for their once-in-a-lifetime hajj, and Christians trekking to Santiago de Compostela in northern Spain are just a few examples. Pilgrimage sites tend to spring up in places where a significant and shared spiritual experience has brought people together in awe, challenge and inspiration — and these people need not have been prominent or powerful. Many of the Roman Catholic pilgrimage sites of the 20th century feature children, illiterate peasants or both in their founding stories: ordinary people having extraordinary experiences of the Divine.

As any pilgrim will tell you, the first thing that they find themselves confronting on pilgrimage is the 'why' for the journey. What did they think they were setting out to sort out, to solve by walking? Travelling long distances on foot at a steady pace brings up all sorts of unsolved things within us. This is the grace of walking: not being able to escape ourselves. If they are willing the pilgrim soon finds that the destination is not half so important as the journey itself, the space it gives, the inner work that's accomplished by just putting one foot in front of another. Little things — a surprise grove of trees along the way, a blister, a conflict with a fellow traveler, a refreshing change from concrete to earthen path — take on a wider significance. Within the journey the pilgrim finds points of resonance with other, larger life experiences. The *why* for the journey is the way itself. But without a destination, why would a pilgrim bother to set out? They wouldn't! This is the first insight that pilgrimage-walking gives to us as urban dwellers: the destination *does* matter, even if the journey's always wilder than we think.

On reaching their destinations, some pilgrims describe a kind of anti-climax. Maybe it's a hunger for more than what that place can give or a sense of exhaustion which gets in the way of whatever big holy or healing moment they'd hoped to have. These frustrations are crucial to the experience of pilgrimage, reminding pilgrims that rarely are any of our life's journeys as linear as we'd like. What a pilgrim receives at their destination is no less a gift for being complicated, confusing, or anti-climactic.

In fact, it is much easier to see our spiritual lives as having a circular or spiral dimension than as following a straight line. The practice of walking slowly around a holy site in a circle is a recurrent theme in spiritual traditions. This allows people to enact this spiritual spiral in a concrete way: to remind themselves that, as T. S. Eliot would famously write, 'in my end is my beginning.' The simple circling walk gave rise to the practice of walking the labyrinth: a more maze-like journey, but a similar intention.

It may sound like I'm saying: on the one hand, pilgrimage is all about the destination, and on the other, it's not about the destination at all. Yep! This is the paradox. It is this paradox, this wrestling with the very idea of destinations, which makes pilgrimage such a rich seam of wisdom for us as urban dwellers. Seeing our urban walking as pilgrimage returns us again to the *why* of our walking, inviting us to approach that paradox and jump in.

Wisdom of the streets

Psychogeography helps teach us about *how* to walk and pilgrimage about *why*. So is the only thing left just...to do it? Yes. The process of un-learning and re-learning how to walk is straightforward but not easy. So much of our way of moving about in the world is something we learned very young, and our walking is conditioned by the pressures we face around *getting somewhere*. To walk a city as a spiritual practice is an exercise in slowing down and paying attention.

A few years ago, I discovered a tool which was incredibly helpful for me as I developed my practice of walking: Street Wisdom. Founded in 2013, this creative social enterprise has sought to empower people around the globe to slow down and listen to their urban landscapes through a series of short walks. At its heart it is a fairly simple and flexible form of walking meditation, gently facilitated by a leader. One of the things I love about it is it is open source: anyone can attend, and anyone can lead.

If you were to attend a Street Wisdom event, you would first gather in a group and meet your fellow walkers. You'd be encouraged to bring a question or a situation in your life for which you'd like some fresh insight. You'd then be sent out on a number of short walks, each with a task to help you slow down and tune in to what's around you in the city. After another quick time together in your group, you would be sent out to take a longer walk, maybe up to an hour. This time, you would hold your question or situation in mind as you walk and see what comes up for you — from within you, and from what you notice around you — in response to that question. A final gathering of your group would give you a chance to share what has come up, in the form of insight, new questions, or anything else.

As with any form of walking meditation, Street Wisdom can be done without a specific question or situation in mind, but I have found having a question or intention gives the walk a much-needed focus. As with most spiritual practices, what you get out of them is often proportional to what you put in. It is easier to notice a resonance or a synchronicity, or what you might call a nudge from God, if you have an intention for those things to resonate with.

When starting out on their first Street Wisdom or other form of intentional urban walking, some folks find the activity baffling. They wonder, 'What am I supposed to pay attention to? Where are these nudges or resonances? Is there some kind of secret code I'm learning here?' Well, if there is a code, I've never learnt it. Mostly these walks are an exercise in building up trust in your own intuition, your own ability to make sense and meaning from the prompts all around you. This is a trust that the right message, insight or meaning will find you when you open yourself up to it, and to the Divine behind it.

Street Wisdom taught me some basics. When you set out walking, first check in with each of your senses. Check in with your body. Then try dropping your pace — see if you can walk only half as fast as you normally would. You might find that you speed up at various points during your walk, which is fine. If you notice you have sped up, just return to a slower pace.

A few things you might find it helpful to pay attention to, once you have slowed down and checked in with your senses and your body:

- *Patterns.* Our minds like patterns and structures. Where do you see patterns around you, in buildings, streets, trees, vehicles, sounds?

- *Intuitive / gut reactions.* Some of us are better than others at listening to our gut reactions. Try focusing in on something or someone on your walk, and listening to what your gut tells you about it or them. What impressions or thoughts come to you? How do those feel in your body?

- *When you feel impatient or irritated.* Spirituality, and especially urban spirituality, makes space for the times we experience negative thoughts or feelings. They can help us know when change is coming. Are you finding something irritating about this walk? Can you sit with that, and listen to what it might be saying?

- *Symbols.* Shop signs, graffiti, the sides of business vans, posters advertising events...graphic symbols are everywhere. Do any of these symbols jump out at you? Why? *Things you find particularly attractive and particularly repellent.* This is related to 'listening to your gut' above, but takes it a step further. Challenge yourself to identify *why* you find something beautiful, or *why* you'd like to avoid something else.

- *Surprises.* Pleasant or unpleasant, surprises jolt us out of our plans and expectations. The holy vulnerability of this jolt is always worth listening to deeply.

If this list seems impossibly long, don't worry. It's not possible to pay attention to all the things on this list at the same time. Treat this list as a sort of map legend for your urban walks: something you can return to again and again to deepen them.

Sacred Pavement: Walking the walk

Each single, simple step taken in the city is one taken on sacred pavement. By this I mean not that the pavement itself is more sacred than any other material, but that because walking is so basic, it is a great place to start as we reconsider our cities as inherently spiritual places. Walking is a deceptively straightforward activity which can help us open our eyes in wonder to our cities, ever places of mystery. Walking is among the spiritual basics, no matter whether you're going about it on your feet, or if you have to use some mobility aid.

Urban Adventures

The adventures at the end of each chapter of this book are intended to be taken slowly — as with walking, always more slowly than you think! Knowing the speed of life and full schedule most city dwellers have, I'd suggest you give yourself plenty of space and time to work through the adventures in each chapter, and to let what you encounter sink in. You don't have to achieve any spiritual brownie points and you certainly won't end this book with a qualification in Urban Spirituality, so there is no rush.

I've called them adventures because of the playfulness and the bravery the word implies. Telling yourself or your flatmate, 'I'm going out now for my adventure' might sound a little silly at first, but why should it? There is no shame in a spirituality that springs from a place of play. After all, play helps us get past the limits our more sensible, rational minds would like to place on us, and returns us to that place of wonder which is so fundamental to a living spirituality.

You'll be encouraged to devote a journal page or two to each of the adventures. Without further ado:

1. *Slowing down.* Look through your schedule for a week and find a time you have to walk between one place and another. You might be going from one site to another for your work, or out to a big supermarket for the weekly groceries, or walking 15 minutes around the corner to visit a friend. Give yourself at least double the time that you need to do this small walk — triple, if you can. Notice how your body reacts to this deliberate slowing down. Do you enjoy it or find it frustrating? What do your senses pick up on this walk that you might have missed if you hadn't chosen to slow down?

   In your journal, give a double-page spread to sketching this walk: the roads or paths you used, the things you noticed or felt. Draw yourself in — stick figures absolutely allowed — and take a moment at the end of the walk to scribble any notes you'd like to reflect on later, in further journalling or a time of meditation.

2. *Symbols & patterns.* Find a time where you can take at least an hour on a walk. Choose an area or neighbourhood to walk in that isn't too quiet, and spend the hour walking and observing the symbols and patterns you see around you. Pause regularly to sketch them in your journal and take at least a page for every one. Bricks in the walls of buildings. Logos on vans or shop-fronts. The shapes made by people swerving around each other on the sidewalk pavements. Do you notice that you are drawn to or repelled by particular symbols? Do any of the patterns make you think of patterns in your own life?

3. *Mini pilgrimage.* Give yourself the gift of a half day walking towards a destination. Is there a bookstore you love, a building of cultural or religious significance, a museum you've never visited though you live fairly nearby? Plan a route that will take you a good 3-4 hours to walk there. Bring a bottle of water and a flask of coffee or tea, and give yourself a break halfway through. In your journal, sketch your route. This could look like an actual map with a bird's-eye view, or it could be a more creative rendering, where you focus on what you find on the way. When I do this exercise I often make both kinds of maps. First I sketch a more or less descriptive map with roads and routes marked, so I get a sense of accomplishment of where I've been. Next, on another page, I note down landmarks, or places where I was met with moments of beauty, confusion, or wonder, and just connect them with a line. This helps me reflect on how I inhabited the walk.

As you walk, have a think about how your destination has shaped your journey. Did it influence what you wear, the route you took, the speed you walked, the companions you chose for the journey?

When you get to the destination, is your experience of it different because you chose to walk there? How so? All of these questions can be used as journal or meditation prompts.

4. *Street Wisdom:* If you found the description of Street Wisdom above interesting, you can go to streetwisdom.org and search for an event near you. You can also download their free leaders' guide if you think you might like to host an event of your own in the future.

CHAPTER 2

Reading architecture

'Oh my god! You're from the 60s. Back to the 60s! Back! There's no place for you here in the future!' If you don't immediately recall this movie quote: it's James Earl Jones playing the writer Terence Mann in the film *Field of Dreams*. His character is bitter and sarcastic and just wants to be left alone. In this scene he's attempting to shoo an earnest Ray Kinsella, played by Kevin Costner, out of his apartment. If you've seen the film, you know that Terence goes on to believe in the project of the *Field of Dreams* even more than Ray does, encouraging him when all seems lost. But at first, encouragement is the last thing on his mind.

When city-dwellers look around them at the architectural styles, many of them seem to have a reaction similar to Terence Mann to architecture of the 20th century, especially that of the 1960s. 'Look at that hideous midcentury tower block!' 'Didn't they have any other materials besides concrete?' 'Everything built after 1930 is basically an eyesore.' 'We should just bulldoze the lot of them and make way for better.' I put these in quote marks because they are comments I overheard on an architecture tour of a central London housing estate during the London Open House festival a few years ago.

I found myself keeping very quiet on this tour because I've always had a soft spot for architecture of this time period, whether it's properly Brutalist or not. Brutalism refers to a particularly simple or even stark style of architecture popular during the 1960s and 70s that uses a lot of exposed steel and *béton brut*, French for unadorned concrete. Brutalism is a style people love to hate. It doesn't offer a lot of comfort or charm in the traditional sense. As with all styles, there are good and bad examples of Brutalist architecture — plenty of apartment blocks which are just pretty dreadful grey monsters.

What endears me to this period in history generally, and the buildings it produced in particular, is that so much of it was so optimistic, even naïve. So many of the high-rises and pedways which are now derided as ugly were intended to create utopian 'cities in the sky', with features intended to improve and simplify the lives of those living or working there. Swiss-French architect Le Corbusier is one of the most famous designers of this era. His tower blocks were devised to include not only comfortable, functional apartments but also shops, restaurants, and other communal spaces and often a school nearby. Naturally no utopian ideal is without its critics: if you want a scathing attack on the idea that a well-built building could somehow create social progress or ascension of the human species, check out J. G. Ballard's novel *High Rise*. Ballard is right, to be sure, that supposedly perfect buildings alone cannot solve the problems of our species. Nevertheless architecture of this era always has a strong ring of hope about it.

In the previous chapter, one of the ways I urged you to interact with your urban environment was through noticing the patterns and symbols all around you, especially in the built environment. Columns, steps, tables set out in a square, lanes for vehicles in the road. Though few of us are urban planners, it doesn't take much effort to start detecting the huge amount of planning — sometimes, conflicting plans — that go into the urban spaces around us. It is often the case that we only notice these plans when they break down. When a bicycle lane ends abruptly just before a massive 4-lane traffic roundabout, the cyclists notice pretty quickly.

We can also go years without truly noticing the buildings around us if we have little reason to access them. For nearly a decade I lived within ten minutes' walk of an amazing feat of Brutalist architecture and never knew it — and here I was, pretending to be a fan of this style. How I came to discover this hidden gem is a story worth telling.

It began in a local bookshop where I found a copy of the *Brutalist London Map*, something clearly designed for anoraks like me. I noted that there was a place called Keeling House fairly nearby but promptly forgot that fact on leaving the bookshop. A few weeks later, my partner and I had gone out for a Saturday morning walk around the neighbourhood. Following our feet down streets we didn't recognise, we ambled along, chatting about funny street names or lovely period windows, at one point turning north towards Hackney down a street we had both passed hundreds of times but never used.

You can guess where this is going. Scarcely a block from the main road, directly in front of us, stood Keeling House, a gorgeous 1950s block of flats, 16 storeys high. I hadn't thought to bring the *Brutalist London* map with me, so we stood at the foot of the gated-off courtyard and entryway with its funky fountain, wondering aloud what the building must be like from the inside. We'd been there about 15 minutes, alternately gazing upward and googling on our phones, when a short, balding bespectacled man walked by us with two armfuls of groceries and stopped.

'Are you architects?' he said. We had to admit that despite our good taste in glasses, we were not. This didn't seem to phase him. He himself was an architect, and he and his partner had bought a flat in Keeling House a few years ago, as they'd always wanted to live in a modernist flat. We asked him a raft of questions about the history of the building, its designer Denys Lasdun and his contemporaries, and what it had been like to see the local neighbourhood change in recent years.

I'm not sure at what point in the conversation it happened, but our new acquaintance decided that he would invite us up for a cup of tea and to have a look around. 'I'll just ring my partner to make sure he's awake and dressed!' he joked. I checked my watch: it was only just 10am. We whizzed through the impeccably weeded courtyard, past its futuristic fountain and up the impressively clean lift very nearly to the top floor. Along the way our host pointed out all the building's features and secrets, a childlike thrill and pride in his voice.

Luckily, his partner was up for receiving two complete strangers into his home on a Saturday morning. We were invited to explore this Rubik's Cube of a flat: compact, angular, and exquisitely designed and fitted together. The wide living room window faced northwest over the ever-changing cityscape. I remember the day being grey and unremarkable: no sun-drenched vista of my beloved London, but an impressive view nonetheless. We stayed for tea and a tour, our new friends delighting us with stories of how they'd managed to scrape pennies together and buy the flat, poring over heavy architecture art books about architecture of that era. *How many people*, I wondered, *have a full colour catalogue of professional art photos about their own apartment block!?*

Eventually it came time to leave them to the rest of their weekend, and so with many thanks we took our leave. We lingered on the outdoor walkways between the flats and the lift, taking photos with bizarre perspectives of the elegant concrete nooks and niches. All at once the breeze picked up, blowing the morning's clouds away and we were drenched in sunlight. The building all but hummed warmly in response. It was time to go.

In the lift, my partner and I completely lost it. We doubled over with grateful laughter at the extraordinary morning we'd just had, all because of a little geeky, nosy wander, and some gracious neighbours. Between the tears of laughter and saying 'Wow, I can't believe that just happened!' over and over again, I'm not sure we had much of a conversation the whole way back home. Since then, the *Brutalist London* map has provided ideas for a great many more adventures in architecture, but none have been quite so exciting or unexpected as that.

Relating to our built environment

Each city has its own architectural treasures, eyesores, and buildings which utterly divide opinion. Part of living out one's spiritual life in a city is learning how to relate to these buildings. If 95% of urban dwellers' lives are spent relating not to mountain vistas and great golden sunsets, but to brick and stone, glass and tarpaulin — then we work with what we've got.

We make a million daily automatic choices of how, and the degree to which, we relate spiritually to what's around us. Many of us — myself included — have a default mode of moving through our everyday lives without a sense of the spiritual in the urban environment around us. Maybe we have a spiritual practice, but we conceptualise it as a thing that we carry with us *through* a rather neutral environment, or an environment we simply assess based on our tastes. But what if the built environment has the capacity to be more than a neutral backdrop? What if we were able to change our perspective?

A helpful image is this. Imagine being in an airplane and coming in for a landing after night has fallen. Looking below to the ground, you're able to see thousands of points of lights are dotted around, some still, some moving. It is easy to think of ourselves as little points of light, beings of spirit, existing on the blank background of our built environment. But what if you happen to be lucky enough to be on that airplane on a clear night, when you can see the city from much farther away, not just that last moment of landing when the plane comes back down through the clouds and the landing gear unfolds. What if, from a hundred miles away, the city shines out before you with all its contours illumined by light, appearing not as a loose association of points of light, but as a greater whole?

There's a name for this discipline of shifting perspective and seeing the greater whole: mapmaking. Mapmaking from a spiritual perspective — what we're doing in this book — is the spiritual discipline of seeing this greater whole and documenting our intentions, questions and adventures within it. As urban dwellers, we can choose to just shrug off the built environment's influence on our moods, thoughts and spirituality. Much more profitably for our spiritual journey, we can relate to the built environment as just as much a living part of our city as flower-boxes, trees and urban wildlife. The human-made slabs and stones are as alive as those boulders which hem in the Grand Canyon, if we have the courage to change our perspective and see it.

Primary wonder

One way in which we can relate to our built environment as a spiritual practice is in how we allow it to nudge us towards wonder. In one of my favourite poems by Denise Levertov, 'Primary Wonder', Levertov marvels that it is possible for humans to forget the 'quiet mystery [...] that there is anything, anything at all...' and that this 'anything' is held in being by a Creator or a 'Hallowed one'. But it is possible, and occasionally even quite fashionable, to forget this quiet mystery, isn't it? If you're reading this book I guess that maybe you've moved on from or never embraced this fashion, or have had experiences which stirred up in you this primary wonder. I reckon that not many of those experiences have involved skyscrapers, though.

In the city, learning to read the buildings around us as a spiritual practice is a part of nurturing this wonder in our daily, concrete realities (pun intended) rather than having to wait for a wilderness. Levertov's poem challenges our human tendency to forget that every moment is a spiritual experience — we are beings of spirit, after all. We are only ever a breath away from that natural impulse to say 'Wow!' to the miracle of existence. For me, learning to interact with the buildings around me is giving myself space to marvel at them, to sense my way towards this *wow* in the here and now. I don't need to wait to be wowed by a mountain on vacation in order to connect back in with that primary wonder which forms part of the taproot of spirituality. Neither do you.

What does it mean to connect to this primary wonder? The life of the Spirit is personal and can be hard to describe without resorting to heavily conceptual, metaphoric language which can feel miles away from our lived realities. It's crucial, then, that we continually re-ground our spiritual lives in our bodies: which is why I began the practical chapters of this book with a chapter on walking, and why embodied spiritual practices like yoga, body prayer, and chanting recur in faith traditions around the world.

Embodying wonder starts with bringing an awareness to what's going on inside us. From there our awareness shifts to what our senses bring us from outside. This is the paradox of embodiment: bodies are both what keeps us separate from everything and everyone else, and the means by which we relate to everyone and everything else. What does wonder feel like in your body? This is a question to mull over and answer to yourself before setting out to understand how the built environment draws you towards wonder. For some people this will be an instantly recognisable feeling: for others who feel first and articulate later, this can take more time. How will you know if you feel it?

Maybe the most accessible way of feeling wonder is when we encounter something we find beautiful. We may be arrested by the sense of simplicity (or complexity), its symmetry (or quirky asymmetry). The colours may be ones we particularly like, or we may like what we feel this thing is trying to say. This is a good way to approach the spiritual practice of reading the architecture around you. Start by finding those buildings or features which you find unequivocally *gorgeous*. They might be great landmarks or they might be doorways you pass everyday on your way to work. Experiencing and revelling in these beautiful things is training in wonder.

A colleague of mine helped me to think more deeply about beauty in the buildings around me one day when we were on our way to a meeting together. On our way through a dense council estate, he said, 'Let's go through this estate this way, and I'll show you where I would love to stage a production of *Romeo and Juliet*.' A former actor, he has a keen eye for performance and a sharp spatial awareness. The courtyard he showed me was of a red brick art deco block of flats; each main door was accessed by a short staircase and little balcony. In a flash, I could see Juliet peeping out from the door, sighing, while her Romeo pined on audience level down in the car park. My colleague excitedly pointed out where he thought the sword fights could be staged, the lovers' flight, the death scene. It was such a joy to watch him delight in a simple council estate which he thought beautiful enough for Shakespeare. The wonder in his voice was unmistakable.

What about the eyesores?

It's one thing to feel into wonder when appreciating beauty in the built environment. It's another thing altogether — though I'd say one just as crucial to the spiritual life — to grapple with what strikes us as ugly or just plain boring. For example: let's return to my love of Brutalism. I'm under no false ideas that everything made of exposed rough concrete is beautiful. On a recent trip to Margate, a seaside town in the southeast of England, I was reminded of this as I walked by the beach-front and found myself saying an audible, 'Blech!' at the sight of Arlington House in all its grey grimness. That such a tall, unkempt and uninspired building should face onto the sea seemed offensive to me, and definitely not beautiful. I did not feel a sense of wonder except perhaps to wonder who on earth had given planning permission for it to be built.

Without a sense of beauty, can we include this experience in the realm of spirituality? I think we can and we must. Wonder is not the sum total of the spiritual journey after all, though it might be an easy way in. Growing in spiritual maturity, however, means slowly and sometimes painstakingly realising that *everything belongs* in the spiritual life: not just our literal or metaphorical mountaintop experiences, not just those times we've been bowled over by beauty or by some other pleasant state of being, such as gratitude or joy. From such moments we are able to easily connect with the Divine so as to better recognise her when she meets us elsewhere.

A spirituality which is limited to good vibes, love and light only repeats the old escapist dilemma which this book is trying to address. It is the dilemma in which many people of faith and spirituality find themselves: the dilemma of only feeling able to inhabit one's spirituality in the good times, or by conjuring something like those good times by escaping the negative or difficult stuff. When we find ourselves facing this dilemma, the ugly buildings in our urban environments are our teachers.

Ugly buildings teach us by offending us. Often our physical reactions to things we find un-lovely are more precise and easier to describe than when we encounter beauty. Experiencing that cringe or disgust may not be pleasant and it may not be a place we want to spend a lot of time, but it is honest. In our spiritual lives, it can be incredibly easy to be dishonest with ourselves: what we think we like, want or need, what guidance we receive, what we might be avoiding. Learning self-honesty can be slow work, and the process of understanding our gut reactions to what we find ugly in our cityscape is part of keeping us honest.

Not only that, but it keeps us asking the honest question about what we find ugly in our own lives. I said above that a recognition that *everything belongs* is a part of spiritual maturity. Naturally, there are going to be aspects of our own lives that don't fill us with wonder, but instead make us cringe. Encountering the ugly in our cityscapes can prompt us to identify those parts of our own lives which we find ugly, and why we find them so. For example, I can be a brilliant procrastinator. I highly value productivity, so it would make sense that one of my besetting vices would be the shadow of this productivity: procrastination. I don't like my tendency towards procrastination. I find it an ugly part of my inner cityscape. And yet, when I really sit down to address my procrastination, really look at what it is and why it is there, I am given huge insight into my inner life, both where I am blocked, and where I could stand to show myself a bit more compassion. When I bother to sit with the ugliness, let it rankle me, and not exclude it from the realm of my spirituality, I'm more likely to be able to shift my attitudes and practices around it.

This is just one example — you'll have your own inner ugly buildings as do we all. They are a part of who we are, and they belong to our spiritual lives. Encountering architecture that we find beautiful *and* ugly helps us do this work: to connect with our bodies, get real about our inner lives, and be continually reminded that *everything belongs,* even and especially the stuff which we'd rather not see. The simplest way to do this — to add a bit more intention into how you interact with the built environment around you — is to find ways to change your point of view.

Changing your point of view

Firstly: slow. down. Cities can be madly hurried places — that's one of their ugliest traits. Changing perspective starts with slowing down enough to realise what your current perspective is. The next step in encountering the built environment is curiosity. I find it helpful to treat the buildings of your urban environment a little bit like Lego creations brought to you by a 3-year-old child. Take a second to delight in them even if you struggle to see their purpose (function isn't everything). Be curious about them, the time and the steps it took to assemble them. Feel free to investigate or imagine what they look like from different angles — literally changing your vantage point.

A few years back I experienced a dramatic change in vantage point which completely changed how I relate to a piece of architecture: London's Tower Bridge. Tower Bridge has never really wow-ed me. I find it garish and I know how frustrating drawbridge traffic (both the vehicles and the tourists) can be! Going to a concert in the Bascule Chamber changed that. This chamber lies beneath the water level of the River Thames; it is the part of the structure which accommodates the counterweights of each side of the drawbridge when it opens up. Although not an engineer, I still found this pretty fascinating. Not only were there actual guides in high vis and hard hats with headlamps leading us down, down, down into the chamber, but we were staying down there for a concert of experimental orchestral music. For a brief moment towards the end of the deliciously eerie final piece, the lights were turned completely off and we held silence together, almost as if we were on a caving expedition in Appalachia, surrounded by stalactites dripping into existence rather than the sound of cars on the bridge and the watery echoes of the river outside.

It may be obvious from my glee at all this that I am not claustrophobic.

After that experience a whole new way of relating to Tower Bridge opened up for me: one of memory, curiosity, and yes, wonder, even though I don't find the bridge beautiful. All this was because I bothered to change my perspective, taking a chance to experience part of the built environment in a new way, to befriend it in a way I hadn't before.

I'll return in Chapter 7 to the importance of seeking hidden places in your city including those which are underground. You need not find ways of going inside the subterranean bits of all your local buildings to accomplish the same shift of perspective, however, or to encounter the built environment of your city with intention. Sometimes it's about just taking a different route, learning a bit of history related to architecture of an area, going on a free walking tour, or finding a way to get a few more storeys up in the air in order to get a more bird's-eye view. You might be surprised how, with a change of perspective, you're able to encounter a building in a whole new way and read a whole different message from it.

Sacred Pavement: Reading architecture

Buildings and the built environment may not be the first thing that spring to most of our minds when we think of the life of the spirit. By chasing our perspectives and giving ourselves space to find beauty in the built environment, and likewise to sit with that which we find unappealing, we allow ourselves to sharpen our spiritual senses of sensual appreciation, playfulness and discomfort, amongst others. Taking time to read architecture — both that which we like and that which we don't — helps us to learn the crucial lesson of spiritual maturity, that *everything belongs.* God is to be found within all our experiences, not just those which are pleasant or pretty. In the next chapter, I'll dig a bit deeper into how we cope with discomfort when it's part of our daily lives, not just an aesthetic preference.

Urban Adventures

I chose the word 'reading' in the title for this chapter specifically because of how it echoes what we might do with sacred texts, images or divinatory tools. To read these buildings is no less important or normal a way to be open to the whispers of Spirit.

Before we start, a check-in: how have you been using your journal? How easy or difficult has it been for you to write, draw and map what you've been up to?

1. *Unshared Photography.* Part of attending to the urban landscape in front of you is to resist the temptation to share everything. Instead, use the tools you have to delight in your urban environment for its own sake, not for the sake of sharing your delight. Identify two bits of architecture in your city — one that you find beautiful or compelling, and one that you find strange or ugly. Take your phone or your camera and spend at least half an hour alone with each of them, taking photos. Don't share any of them online anywhere. These photos are your prayerful conversation with your environment: use them as starting points for meditation or for journaling. How has taking these photos helped you change your point of view? Where are the places of resonance or dissonance between what you observe and your own inner life? Did anything surprise you? In what ways can you tell that your urban environment shapes your interaction with the Divine?

   If you want to get even more retro with this adventure, try limiting the number of photos you can take by buying a disposable camera with only 24 exposures on it. Yes, there are places that you can still get film developed!

2. *Speed-sketching.* Find two buildings (different to the ones you chose for the first adventure) that elicit strong reactions in you whether positive, negative or mixed. Dedicate a two-page spread in your journal to each. Set a timer, and give yourself 2 minutes to sit or stand near the building and sketch it. Do this on the left side of the page in as much detail as you can. Once the timer goes — that's it. Pen down. Set the timer again for 2 minutes, and use the other side of the page to journal in as unfiltered a way about what this building brings up for you. What words do you associate with it? What symbols? Where else do these symbols appear for you in your inner life, your work, your relationships? Once the two minutes are up (or you've filled the page!), you're done.

You can choose to do this with more than two buildings, or to incorporate it into a more regular prayer or meditation practice. Resist the desire to give yourself more time for either the sketching or the journalling — the key to this is listening to those instant, sometimes bizarre, associative images and thoughts which can often give us a new perspective on the contours of our own spiritual life.

3. *Draw yourself as a building.* This is one for all those who grew up playing computer games where you had to build cities or towers, creating a little urban ecosystem. Imagine yourself as one of the buildings in your city — or if that's too complicated,

a generic building. Where is the emotional centre located? The 'spirituality department'? The communications team? Where does the nourishment come from and how does the building get cleaned? Remembering that everything belongs, don't forget to add into this drawing those parts of yourself you don't like so much. (For me, I'd need a whole floor for the Procrastination Department!)

4. *Free spaces.* If you've spent time unemployed or studying in a city you'll know how important it is to find those free and cheap places to be if you want to afford going out! Research some of those spaces in your city — parks, libraries, galleries, etc. — and pay a few of them a visit, sketching and describing them in your journal. How is the architecture of these community-focused spaces different to other aspects of the built environment? How do they 'read' differently? What spiritual lessons about accessibility, hospitality, and kindness do they offer you, if any?

CHAPTER 3

The Commute

'It doesn't look very far as the crow flies,' I said to my flatmate as we huddled together over the computer screen, open to Google maps.

'Is that another one of your weird Americanisms?' he asked. 'I think we have ravens here in London, not crows.'

I bit back a sarcastic quip about the six ravens kept un-flying, wings clipped, at the Tower of London, the loss of which will result in the fall of Britain and its monarchy according to popular legend. Instead I said, 'As the *raven* flies, then. In a straight line, it doesn't look far. How bad do you think it can be to cycle it?'

As it turned out, cycling from the one side of London to another, less than four miles, was a bit like putting a puzzle together when you weren't sure what the final picture was supposed to look like. Even these days, as Transport for London has continually worked to improve its infrastructure for cyclists, cycle-commuting can be a piecemeal affair. My flatmate and I worked out a couple of potential routes to the best of our ability, taking into account the patterns of morning traffic and sites of current road works. Some congested streets were unavoidable (my office was just off Parliament Square) but on the whole we devised a pretty decent route to work.

On my first day, I hopped on my bike at 7:45am and got less than a mile away before I decided this route was a complete disaster. The roads I'd expected to be full only of taxis and buses were bumper-to-bumper with every cyclist's nemesis: lorries. Lorries galore. There was an unexpected lane closure and several scary-looking right turns to make (in a land where you drive on the left, the right-hand turns can make your life flash before your eyes). Just as I began to lose my nerve, I realised my failure to make it into a right-hand turn lane had landed me onto the approach to London Bridge. Before I knew it I was powering up the incline, passing parked busses as they waited next to the Monument to the Great Fire of London. I discovered that day what I have often tried to describe since: the great pleasure of crossing London Bridge southward on a bicycle.

Cycling over the bridge, you're going faster than on foot, so you have a sense of the currents of wind and weather. You're not enclosed in a car or a bus, so despite the traffic noise, there's an odd quiet that falls when you get out over the water, once the sound isn't trapped between buildings. To your left is Tower Bridge in all its Disney-ish Victorian splendour. To your right the river curves, the Victoria Embankment lining it with elegant trees. In front of you the Shard juts upward, dwarfing the wharves amongst which Southwark Cathedral and Borough Market are nestled, just waking up for the day.

No matter how many times I've made the crossing, no matter what the weather, it takes my breath away a bit — and not just because I'm cycling uphill! Besides the joy of saying hello to all the landmarks is a little thrill of excitement that I am going over a living river which has seen thousands of years of human life in this place, and aeons more before that. That day, as I took a rather more roundabout route than expected to my new job, I felt not only the joy and wonder of this crossing, but also a great deal of gratitude that this could be my commute. A necessary joy. That route became the one I took most days, crossing over London Bridge, wiggling through Southwark, and coming back over Westminster Bridge to pass by Big Ben — if I was lucky, while it was chiming the half-hour.

Most London commuters I know would absolutely not describe their commute as a necessary joy. In fact, many will have a story of a nightmare commute. Maybe it's one they did just for a weeklong gig, maybe one they endured for years. In London, the Underground is the chief culprit for these stories. Known as the 'Tube' because of its curved tunnels and trains, a rush-hour experience there can really give the feeling of being squeezed through the bowels of the city. London isn't unique — or even the worst — in this respect. The videos of Tokyo's underground are legendary for their sardine-tin effect. On the mostly-silent, mostly well-behaved London underground, the fear of having to spend 20 minutes every morning with your nose stuck in a stranger's armpit is enough to make many people become cyclists, or try to get in to work much earlier in the day.

These crowded experiences are not limited to underground transport. Both colleagues with whom I shared my Westminster office commuted about an hour to work by train from south London. A good day was when they got a seat for at least part of the journey. When they arrived already a bit squashed-looking at 9, I knew to put the kettle on right away so they could plop down in their office chairs and take tea and a breather before the work day even began.

A spirituality of commuting?

The sheer blessing of enjoying at least one aspect of my commute to work has caused me to reflect on the crossover of spirituality and work life, especially the getting-to-and-from-work part. I've heard faith leaders from various traditions encourage people to maximise the time they spend on the train, in the car, or on foot by praying, listening to podcasts or reading books that will support them in their inner life. Recently I came across a podcast which consists solely of two voices praying the words of the Rosary with all its daily and seasonal variations, presumably so Christians could follow along with beads on a crowded bus. I know Buddhists who have particular mantras for their journeys and New Agers who carry specific crystals to ground and protect them. As I write this chapter, the month of Ramadan is just beginning, and on the tube this morning I saw at least one person following along in a book of Islamic devotions.

All these are great strategies of adding or weaving in a spiritual practice into what can often be a less-than-pleasant experience of commuting. But what about the big picture, the commute itself? Can that regular journey be in itself a spiritual activity, or do we have to cram spirituality into it? I believe it can if we make the space to learn some of the spiritual lessons it offers to our lives as a whole, lessons around discomfort, discipline and dependence.

Discomfort

Once a year in the greyest weeks of January in London, there is an event which fills many commuters with horror: the Annual No Trousers Tube Ride. Based on a similar event which began in New York City in the early 2000's, the purpose of the day is pretty clear: to ride the tube with no trousers on, at rush hour or otherwise. The event organisers issue amusing guidance for those taking part: 'please avoid particularly skimpy underwear; please aim to amuse — not embarrass — your fellow commuters.' Having never quite worked up the bravery to take part in this event, it nevertheless makes me laugh with surprise every time it comes around. The UK in January is not a situation where one might expect bare legs on public transport. The awkwardness of commuting seems to increase ten-fold on that day and the sense of relief is palpable on the next. The discomfort of community remains, however, despite the relief.

Whether your commute is on a crowded bus or train, or takes you on a strenuous cycle ride or through mind-numbing traffic deadlock, there's likely to be some discomfort about it. From the perspective of spirituality, discomfort is a part of any spiritual practice. Getting pins and needles, the 'monkey mind' which won't focus on prayer, the frustrations and messiness of other people in shared faith spaces, the lack of *results* in the intentions we set. No matter the amount of thoughts and prayers, love and light we wish for ourselves and for each other, the fact of the matter is that the spiritual life has its share of difficulty and discomfort. But we keep at it, don't we, sometimes pushing through the discomfort, sometimes letting it pass through us so we can learn from it. In commuting there is plenty of this, which is precisely why it can become a spiritual practice. We learn to recognise that discomfort is not pain and that frustration will not be the end of us, however distracting it may be in the moment. Treating a commute as a spiritual practice gives us a chance to practice some of these lessons in real time.

Discipline

A common buzz-phrase amongst spirituality circles these days is 'showing up.' This can refer to regular presence on social media if you are using that platform to foster some kind of community. As a bigger concept, showing up is about showing up not only to your community but to yourself: forming habits which can foster spiritual growth. The very un-trendy, un-buzzy word behind all this is 'discipline', the dedication it takes to *just keep showing up*.

With commuting, the discipline comes from the job you're going *to* — you are pulled into a habit rather than choosing it, pushing yourself to form it. That doesn't mean, however, that the habit of commuting can't be just as spiritual a practice as sitting down on the meditation cushion. If we were to embrace commuting as a spiritual practice, rather than just a time we need to fill with work or worthy activities, we would be able to recognise the inherent value in this time rather than view it as lost. After all, many people spend more time on the train, bus, bike or car than they do in an explicitly spiritual practice every day.

The discipline of commuting can instil in us an ability to see where discipline is strong, or not so strong, in the rest of our lives. In her book *Holy Spokes*, Laura Everett writes about her cycle commute through Boston, Massachusetts. Everett writes that climbing a steep hill in Boston was a useful measure of her physical health: when she struggled to stay on the bike all the way up, she knew she hadn't been as regular as she would like with her physical exercise. When she was able to zip right up it, the opposite was true.

Discipline isn't a word that belongs only to highly structured systems of faith, to conservative social groups, or to a capitalist work ethic. Discipline is not a dogma. The discipline that regular work (for others and for ourselves) and commuting draws out of us is a glimpse of something deeper than any system of belief or ideology we might assent to with our brains. To put it another way, our habits reveal something of our hearts. This isn't to say that if you don't have the discipline for a long daily commute that there is something wrong with your heart. It is only to point out that who we are at the deepest level is shaped by the habits that fill our days, and habits can be difficult to shift, indeed.

Treating our commutes as a spiritual discipline makes space for us to become aware of those other habits that shape us, maybe those we haven't been pulled into by a job but fallen into almost by accident, maybe those that we have chosen to pursue. It makes us aware of how the habits of our cultures shape our own, and to what degree we have a say in shifting those wider, more communal habits. Commuting as a spiritual discipline insists that we have a responsibility for our habits, whether we feel we've chosen them or they've chosen us.

Dependence

Although some of us might think of a daily commute as being alone in a car, for others a commute is an incredibly social (if not sociable) experience. Even those alone in their cars are incredibly dependent on others for the infrastructure of commuting to work: other drivers on the road or those who design, commission and regularly repair motorways and parking facilities, to name just a few. Commuting is a spiritual exercise in dependence on others. We might depend on the weather, the trains, the mood of the bus-driver or whether someone has been ill on a platform and caused a delay.

It has often been said that realising our dependence on things we can't control is one of the primary lessons of the spiritual life. We are woven into a web of dependency on others, on the whole of this complex ecosystem of earth, and essentially on the Divine. The initial realisation of our dependence can leave us feeling angry, scared or powerless. When accepted and embraced, however, it is a boundless source of empathy and generosity.

No matter how disciplined we seek to be, the Spirit usually works to its own logic. One of the most hopeful and also frustrating bits in the Jewish and Christian scriptures mentions the voice of God saying, 'My thoughts are not your thoughts, neither are your ways my ways'. That divine utterance is an acknowledgement of humanity's inability to reckon on Divine timing, divine logic: our utter dependence, our lack of ability to thrive in isolation.

We can't know everything and everyone on whom we depend at any given moment in time. There is a great liberation,

I believe, in knowing that it is not just ourselves. There is great encouragement in knowing that all of humanity — all of the earth in fact — is in a similar state. Commuting is a picture, a microcosm, of this universal dependence or interdependence. Contemporary urban dwellers have a particularly vivid and diverse picture of this dependence in front of them, every time they step out their door to commute.

Sacred Pavement: Commuting

It's often in our least comfortable moments that we learn the most lasting lessons. Without trying to cram into commuting a raft of explicitly spiritual practices, the practice of commuting itself can teach us some of those lessons which will ground and shape the rest of our lives in deeply spiritual ways. The discomfort of commuting can teach us something about the persistence and maturity of the spiritual journey. The discipline of commuting can teach us about our own responsibility for our habits at heart level. The dependence of commuting can teach us about our wider dependence on one another and on the Divine. Rather than just trying to log these lessons in our brains as inspirational thoughts, we're offered a chance to enact them and let them soak into us, when we choose to treat our commute as a spiritual practice.

Urban Adventures

1. *Hone in on the habit.* Sit down with your journal and sketch out your commute. Get as detailed as you can. What do you pass along the way? What means of transport do you use? Have you developed any routes, tricks or hacks to make your commute more enjoyable, and why? Take a moment to reflect on the three points of this chapter — discomfort, discipline and dependence — in the context of the commute you have drawn.

   Wait until you've done this commute again, and then sit back down and re-sketch it. What did you notice this time that you didn't before?

   A variation on this adventure is do a commute for a previous gig or job that you haven't done in a while, and see what about it you can still do 'with your eyes closed.' What strikes you anew?

2. *Do your normal commute* — do this route at a different time of day than you normally do. How does this change the experience of this travel? What is newly pleasant where there was discomfort, or the other way around?

3. *The necessaries.* In your journal, mind-map out what disciplines your work pattern requires of you. What time do you have to get up before work? How does your commute affect your family members or those you live with? If you work from home, what habits and patterns do you put in the day? Do these disciplines feel like you chose and shaped them, or they chose you?

4. *Dependables.* Make a list of all the people who had to do something to make your commute possible. The person who invented steam trains, so that electric trains might follow. The drivers. The musician who wrote the music you listened to on your earphones as you walked from one place to the other. The builders who laid the pavement stones in such a way that the rain puddles are minimal. Get creative here! This list is a prayer of gratitude and dependence — use it in a time of meditation, if you'd find that helpful.

CHAPTER 4

Thrift & Abundance

I long to become the sort of person who can build a bike from scratch and repair it competently until the bike becomes a patchwork of stories: this handlebar, those wheels, that saddle. Wouldn't that be a cheerful Frankenstein's monster of a bike? So far, however, my record with bikes hasn't been great. Broken frames, thefts in broad daylight, secondhand parts so heavy they belonged on much sturdier mountain-going contraptions — such has been my luck. At least I've some brilliant stories to tell, though, like the time, two days after a particularly gutting theft of a bike which had been entirely gifted to me, I was checking my email and noticed an announcement:

'DO YOU WANT TO BUY STOLEN GOODS!??'

The Metropolitan Police, it seems, have a veritable treasure trove of stolen goods they have recovered in the course of their work. It is apparently more difficult that you'd think to track down the original owners of these goods. After two years gathering dust in a police warehouse, the items are legally up for grabs. The announcement I had read came from the Police, advertising a sale in an old defunct brewery-turned-pop-up-space just around the corner from where I lived.

I went without thinking I would find anything and came home with the most exciting bike I have owned to date: a shiny Cannondale, usually far beyond my price range but hugely discounted. Light as a feather, with drop handlebars and clip-in pedals which I'd have to replace because I'm definitely not professional enough to own clip-in cycle shoes. I walked the bike home, completely giddy with my luck and timing and the excellent deal. *How do I deserve something this nice?* echoed like a quizzical mantra around in my head.

It has taken many years, prayers and conversations to begin to unravel my own beliefs around being worthy. I imagine that's true for many of you reading this book, too. On one hand, I really bristle at the insinuation that I or anyone else could be less than worthy, less than deserving of nice things, a peaceful life, the joy of meaningful relationships. On the other hand, it can be devilishly hard to believe in, and act on, one's personal worthiness.

For a long time I made a virtue out of my thriftiness because I believed I couldn't have nice things. To be honest, I still do enjoy the smugness of saving money. There are endless fun and innovative ways to be thrifty, to reduce my impact on the planet and on my bank balance by buying second-hand, seeking out good deals, sharing and so forth. These are virtuous activities, and I never want to lose sight of the fact that I am immensely privileged these days to be able to *choose* to do them, not be always forced into them by my life circumstances.

On the flip side of every virtue is a vice, however. The flip side of thriftiness and sharing is penny-pinching and being completely ruled by fears of scarcity, and I'm not proud to admit that I have spent plenty of years there. It is easy to justify this mindset, especially if you've ever had periods of your life where money was tight and you had to be immensely responsible with your personal or family budget to stay afloat. The stress of temporary or persistent poverty has been shown to alter the way the human brain works over time — something which might seem obvious but needs stating nonetheless. Whether you have spent time in actual poverty or not, it can be easy to get stuck in a space of scarcity, where it's difficult to believe or trust firstly that you might be worthy of abundance, and secondly that you might be able to reach out for it.

Over the years I've spent living in urban areas, I have been lucky to meet many people who value thrift, sharing and prudence with regard to our resources, and do so from a spirituality of abundance. Some of these friends have been relatively wealthy, others not at all. Just in case it's taking you a while to find those people, let me assure you, they are out there to be found!

Money, money, money

After the financial crisis of 2008, the UK government started to enter into a period described as 'austerity.' This was intended as a temporary measure to stave off the worst of the crisis. It lasted ten years. For me personally, the timing was rotten. 2008 was the year I began to settle into east London and to come into my own as an adult. Public services were being cut, people I knew were going hungry, and I was bringing home about £300 a month. It was a pinched time, and if I wanted to have any kind of life I needed to get really good at finding cheap and free things to do and creative ways to live within my means.

I chose to stick it out in London rather than head somewhere my cash would go further. Is it a bit silly to stay in a city when life is more expensive there? Perhaps. I know plenty of people who, because of wanting to live a life which is generally more relaxed about money, have moved out of urban areas. There have been many times in which I questioned whether my love for my city was deafening me to my own desires for less financial stress. I, like many people, had been pulled to the city by an opportunity and by the urban buzz. Cities are magnetic, offering many ways to work, a world of new and diverse people to meet, ideas to encounter and activities to try. If you aren't pulled there, you may be unable to leave because of jobs, family or property. The matter of leaving a city in order to have less financial stress is usually more complex than just hiring a removal van and setting out for the hills.

For those who do remain in the city despite the increased expense, sharing about spending and about tips on how to stretch money further has become de rigeur, enabled greatly by the internet. Journalist Jack Monroe's *Cooking on a Bootstrap* was a hugely popular online column-turned-cookbook which emerged from this 'austerity' time, boasting recipes that never cost more than £1 per person, each penny assiduously documented. Though it has been more than a decade since the 2008 crisis, online articles that get the most clicks (and most divisive commentary) are those about money and spending. For example, the Money Diaries that profile a person's spending for a week of time. Living within a predominantly capitalist culture, we are fixed on how people spend. But is the slogan true that 'you are what you buy?' To some extent, perhaps, it is.

Where you put your resources is where you put your energy; it is the direction you're likely to go and grow. So where does that leave many cash-strapped urban dwellers? When you can't buy all that much, who are you?

Answer: you probably become someone who shares. Apps and community initiatives for sharing flourish in urban areas, making it possible to borrow tools, toys, cars, workspaces, flats, books...the list goes on. The necessity of sharing is lodged firmly into the urban imagination. Just recently I saw London Underground tunnels plastered with posters advertising a comedy novel entitled *The Flat Share*. The plot: two people share a flat, but due to their working arrangements never meet. Beyond sharing in a literal sense, city dwellers have countless opportunities to be intentional about their spending for the sake of their own finances but also the welfare of others and of the planet. Local currencies, shops which encourage bulk buying, and urban farm schemes are just a few of these. Instead of a purely individualistic 'you are what you buy', city-dwelling offers an option to buy and consume more communally, ethically and mindfully.

A spirituality of money

What does our attitude towards money and financial resources have to do with spirituality? Reams and reams of advice on money, spending, providing for those with less and shrewd management have emerged from the world's faith traditions — most of which did not emerge from cultures informed by the kind of capitalism in which we live today! This leads me to think that financial resources and our attitudes toward them are inherently part of our spiritual lives, just as much are our bodies, our prayer practices, or our communities of support. Money is, when all is said and done, a concept: a way we shape and condition our societies. It's a concept we pretty much all buy into, and it affects most areas of our lives to some degree. Because our relationship to our finances is so far-reaching, it's important we don't make the mistake of thinking we can spiritually bypass it or ignore it completely.

I began this chapter by telling you a little of the journey I'm still on with regard to money. I wouldn't for a second like you to think that I've got this whole abundance thing sorted: not in the slightest. What I have been able to do, thanks to years of urban living which demanded careful attention to my finances, is start interrogating the stories I used to tell myself about money. The word 'interrogate' brings to mind a dark room and a small bright light aimed at your face by a shouty man... and I'd be lying if sometimes, peeling back the layers on layers of harmful stories I learned to tell myself about money didn't feel a little like that! But in time, and with the help of my neighbours, I began learning to ask myself the questions, to pull back the layers, with a bit more kindness. To pray, even, about my relationship with my finances, rather than let my old stories control me.

Thrift or scarcity?

I've already confessed that I do enjoy the thrill of a good deal, and I love a well-stocked thrift or vintage shop. Macklemore's 'Thrift Shop' song will never not be an anthem of mine, but learning the difference between thrift and scarcity has been crucial for me along the way. Thriftiness is a value of saving, sharing, and innovating ways to *use less*. I think it's a crucial part of living well on this Earth. Being forced into these behaviours by city-dwelling isn't always pleasant at first, but in the end I think it can lend itself to great creativity. Practicing thrift can help us root our spiritualities of money in a place that can appreciate luxury as well as restraint: one that can take joy in simplicity and discovering our interconnectedness with all life. (There's that dependence again!)

Practicing scarcity, on the other hand, does slow and steady harm. It results in an anxious worrying about not only money but all resources, and is founded in a belief that what one has will never be enough, because it could (and probably will) be taken away imminently. Scarcity has the side effect of making us highly judgmental towards others about their use of money and other resources. Often it lends itself to angry and warped understandings of who is and isn't 'worthy' or 'deserving' of wealth or poverty, including ourselves. Scarcity isn't something only those with limited resources fall into; in fact, some of the people with the strongest scarcity-practices I know are those with significant material wealth, having profited from the supply-and-demand market which relies on beliefs of scarcity to exist.

Depicting a spirituality of thrift and a spirituality of scarcity as binaries is an oversimplification; most of us aren't clearly practicing just one or the other but are somewhere in the middle, continuing to untangle the ideas about money that we've picked up over our lives. What I'm inviting you to do is to interrogate your ideas kindly, and ask yourself in what ways you find it easy to slide away from thrift (where material enough-ness is found in shrewdness and sharing) and towards scarcity (where there will never be enough).

There's a hilarious episode of the classic British sitcom *Blackadder* in which Edmund Blackadder, the protagonist who is at this time living during the Elizabethan Era, is visited by his intensely grumpy and pleasure-hating Puritan relatives, the Whiteadders. They refuse to drink beer, prefer to sit on spikes and eat nothing but raw turnips. You don't need to be familiar with the show to know what it's mocking here: a certain category of individual who, for reasons of personality or religion or politics or all three, seems incapable of enjoying the good things in life, even when they are handed to them on a platter. This is a caricature — humorous but still important to note — of what happens when we get stuck in scarcity.

Abundance or excess?

When money isn't scarce, we have another choice to make about how we relate to it.

A healthy attitude to money is one of abundance, which looks like wholehearted appreciation for financial resources and our ability to make and use money well. The opposite of abundance is excess: being caught up in a cycle of obsession with financial resources, being overtaken by a belief that 'more is more'.

Maybe some of you have been in the position where plenty of resources taught you that money can't buy happiness; maybe others of you have rarely been in the position of having much extra at all. No matter your experience of money — when it comes your way, you have to choose how to relate to it. Your choice is between an attitude of abundance or one of excess. Abundance is appreciating money when you have it, not refusing to use it, whereas excess is irresponsible and erratic spending. Abundance is knowing the difference between rewarding yourself because you know you're worthy, and spending needlessly to make yourself feel worthy (the latter is excess, too). Abundance is working for and asking for what you want and need financially, knowing you have a role to play in these things coming to you. Excess is expecting a million pounds to land in your lap without any effort on your part, or hoarding your resources long past the point of plenty.

Excess and scarcity are two sides of the same coin, or perhaps two halves of a self-fulfilling cycle. Practicing a spirituality of scarcity leads to excessive behaviour with money when you manage to get a hold of some, which makes you feel like money is scarce when it runs out. Thrift and abundance complete a similar cycle. Practicing a spirituality of thrift lends itself to a greater appreciation of abundance, which in turn encourages some thrift as well as healthy use of resources. That isn't to say that you'll never be surprised by a financial loss or a gift, or that if you engage in practices of abundance, you'll never feel like your resources are really stretched and scarce. It also isn't to say that if you find yourself drifting towards excess in one area of life you won't be able to be thrifty in another. Spiritual economics isn't a zero sum game.

Fundamentally, cultivating a spirituality of abundance with regards to our financial resources is easier in urban city areas because we can see how much our abundance (or lack of it) impacts on others. True abundance is always asking to be shared: this is what generosity means. In cities perhaps more than anywhere else, the opportunities for and the need for generous ways of living are plain everywhere we look.

Sacred Pavement: Thrift & abundance

Throughout this chapter I've persistently used the word 'spirituality' with regard to beliefs and practices around financial resources, even though the practices I've been talking about don't sound very 'spiritual.' No mention of a meditation cushion, candles or prayers — just buying, saving and budget sheets. How do all these words belong in the same sentence? What does it mean to 'adopt a posture of abundance' anyway?

I'm assuming not many of you reading this book will be monks or nuns who've chosen the path of complete renunciation of worldly goods as part of your spirituality of money — and that's fine. (A warm hello to my monastic friends if you're there!) For those of us on a different path, a little daily effort towards practicing thrift and abundance goes a long way. There are ever more helpful apps for saving and sharing goods and tools that can be easily used in urban settings. Practically, having a daily or weekly check in with your finances and asking yourself what you need to practice thrift and abundance is a great place to start. Ask yourself the question 'What would it look like if I were generous towards myself and others with my finances this week / month / year?' Be gentle but honest in your reflections and look for times in which you've slipped into scarcity or excess without meaning to.

These are just a few suggestions — there are probably hundreds of ways you could harness your urban experience to help you unravel and interrogate some of your money stories. You're definitely encouraged to be creative in discovering them. Below are a few ways I've used to do some of this work, first in conversation with myself and then with others. Journal at the ready!

Urban Adventures

1. *One person's trash is another person's treasure.* This is the spiritual practice of secondhand shopping as paying more attention. Take yourself out on a thrift shopping trip and draw it up after! What did you find yourself drawn to? Did you struggle to find things you think were 'worthy of you' there? Sketch pictures of some of the items and label them with adjectives. Notice whether they seem to point to a mindset of thrift or scarcity.

2. *House sharing.* Do you know or have you shared living space before, besides in your home as a child? Sketch out the house, mapping the space and who it 'belonged' to or who spent their time in each room, what space was public and private. Did you get on with your housemates, or not so much? Did sharing a house give you specific opportunities to practice thrift and/or abundance?

3. *Abundance & generosity.* Investigate and map out some local charities in your journal, perhaps drawing a map of the area and putting them on it. Why do you think those charities sprang up in those areas? Think about one you feel particularly

passionate about, and think/plan about what you could give to them: money, time, publicity, another form of gift? How could your abundance support theirs?

4. *Paying it forward.* Buy a coffee for someone behind you in the line at a cafe. Do you think of generosity as something which could be a 'spiritual practice'? Why or why not?

5. *Where has all the money gone?* If you've never done it before, keeping a money diary for a week and tracking every bit of money you spend, can be hugely illuminating. Perhaps keep track for one week in your journal, and take note of your gut feelings around spending. Does spending a little — or a lot — bring up anything for you about your approaches to money?

CHAPTER 5

Neighbourliness

'Won't you be my neighbour?' sang Fred Rogers. His unique brand of comforting, cardigan-wearing, child-friendly twee will always have a special place in my heart. The TV show *Mister Rogers' Neighborhood* was a staple of after-school viewing when I was a young child in America. Long after I grew past its target age demographic I appreciated how he made often difficult or complex topics accessible for children: things like grief, change, joy, betrayal, and accountability. For those of you who aren't familiar with this show, each episode began with Mr Rogers arriving home, changing from a work coat and shoes into slippers and a cardigan, all while singing, *'It's a beautiful day in this neighbourhood… Won't you be my neighbour?'* I'm not sure I've ever lived in the sort of idyllic suburban neighbourhood that Mr Rogers seemed to inhabit, but something about the potential for human care, delight and cohesiveness of the 'neighbourhood' still lodged itself deep within me from a young age.

With this in the background of my brain, it was jarring to relocate to London, a city not known for its effusive neighbourliness. I've met many people from the North of England who bemoan 'the big chill' of London, arguing that the North might have worse weather but far warmer hearts. A few years ago, a campaign called 'Talk to Me London' encouraged people to wear badges with these words on them and willingly start up conversations. The press that this initiative received would have been hilarious if it weren't so sad: 'Yes, London is an unfriendly city — and long may it stay that way,' proclaimed one newspaper headline. In the subtitle, 'Most of us moved here to avoid having to chat to strangers.'

Well cheerio, then.

I get it, really. Living in a city, you can potentially come into contact with dozens if not hundreds of faces just in the course of one commute or trip to the supermarket. It's exhausting and nigh-on impossible to engage meaningfully with each of those faces. For the sake of our sanity, city-dwellers zone out, or put in earphones, looking anywhere but in people's eyes, just getting where we're going as fast as we can.

An unintended consequence of this very necessary self-preservation is that it spills over into the rest of our lives and becomes isolation from those with whom we share space and proximity quite regularly. Moreover, cities are places of great transience. The next-door neighbour you might have just about struck up a first-name relationship with after two years of living 20 feet from each other may find themselves moving to a different place — hopefully not just because you got to know them.

It's not hard to meet people in cities. Part of the allure of urban life is the ease with which one can explore new things and connect with new people: playing a sport, learning a language, going to weird interactive theatre shows, taking a tour, attending workshops. But these things are rather different to actually getting to know your neighbours. At these activities, you make acquaintances who may become friends: people who share an interest and with whom you might connect with ease. Neighbours, though? They can be the last people you *want* to connect with. People with whom you might not have so much in common. So why bother? You've already got too many people in your life that you are trying to keep up with, right? Think again.

Why bother?

Bothering to get to know your neighbours is one of those urban spiritual practices which, depending on your personality and cultural background, can feel incredibly ease-filled and life-giving or painfully awkward and cringey. The beautiful thing about it, as with any spiritual practice, is that you start from where you are, as you are. You aren't expected to suddenly become Mister Gregarious hosting bi-monthly Block Barbecues if that's not your style. The saying about the spiritual life, *Pray as you can, not as you can't,* holds for the practice of getting to know your neighbours as well. Be neighbourly in the ways that you can. You are not required to become someone else, only to test the boundaries of your comfort zone.

But *why*? Why, when the city is so transient, fragmented, diverse and busy, am I insisting that the random collection people you happen to live near have some sort of special status in the arena of your acquaintances? In short my answer is '*Why not?*', but I'll flesh that out a little.

Neighbours are people you have to share with: you share a street, maybe a hallway, probably a rubbish collection day. Perhaps you share a pained look in the morning when a car alarm in the street below went off at 2am and took 15 minutes to deactivate. It is easy to commiserate, isn't it? Some of our most unlikely bonds are forged during times of shared challenges. My question is: what if the bonds that we forge with those geographically nearest us could be forged from a place of good will rather than complaint? What if the boring fact of living near someone gives us an opportunity to reap the benefits of connecting with other living, breathing beings? What if these other beings' difference to us was an occasion for curiosity rather than writing them off outright?

I ask these questions to give you a means of checking in with yourself as urban dwellers. As I wrote above, it can be easy — it can look like self preservation — to knuckle down and limit our interactions with the people around us. But at some point this becomes a habit of avoidance. It is spiritually deleterious, I believe, always to avoid seeing other gorgeous, complex beings face-to-face. As many of the great contemplative traditions remind us, the degree to which we are willing to encounter others, especially those most difficult or different to us, is the degree to which we are willing to encounter the Divine. If we go about our urban lives avoiding those people alongside whom we carry out our lives, our spiritualities suffer for the simple reason that the Divine meets us, at least partially, in those people. There are experiences of God to be had through our interactions with our neighbours that we will never have on a meditation cushion, and lessons to be learnt in listening which can never be condensed into mantras.

Our neighbours are given to us, as we are to them, for a time. We have the ability to shrug at this gift and go about our lives, connecting with only those who are similar to us, or we can choose to open the gift and see what God might have for us, in them. The individual and collective benefits are ours to discover.

Seeking the welfare of the city

Deep down, the spiritual life is not solely about an individual and their relationship to the Divine. That may be where we begin and where we do a lot of the spiritual work, but it is not the goal or the destination. The spiritual path always takes us beyond this me-and-god dynamic to the other lives with whom we share this life and this planet. There's always a tension, in faith and spirituality, between individual and collective. For a long time Western cultures have highly valued the individual over the collective, for some important historical and spiritual reasons. We would do well, however, to recover the importance of the collective in our spiritualities today, especially when that collective includes others whose belief systems or practices are different to our own.

There is a passage from the Jewish scriptures, namely the prophet Jeremiah, which illustrates this point well. The context is this: a large part of the ancient Jewish people have been taken from their homes into exile, with no certain hope of return. Practicing their own faith was tricky in an unfamiliar context, not to mention the conflict and trauma cascading through their communities after such violent war, conquest and displacement.

Into this tumult the prophet says, in a moment of rare encouragement, 'Seek the welfare of the city where you have been brought into exile, and pray to the LORD on its behalf, for in its welfare you will find your welfare.' It is perhaps difficult for us to understand how challenging this statement would have been to its original hearers. They were refugees forcibly enslaved in a land and city not their own amongst people they did not know. What's more, a huge part of the history of the Jewish people had been about coming into their own corporate identity over and against other identities, other peoples, other nations. Here is this prophet, urging them to live peaceably in this city, to seek its welfare, to pray for it and its inhabitants. Prayer and activity, as always, are entwined.

There is a deep insight here into the spirituality of urban life, even if we haven't been carted off to a foreign city against our will by an invading army. To live our spiritualities is to seek each others' good and welfare for their sake, by listening to them and not assuming what we know is good for them. The easiest others to listen to are those nearby, those with whom our daily welfare is most obviously bound up: our neighbours. Maybe even the neighbours we find it least easy to like.

What I am insisting on here is a spirituality of interdependence with our neighbours. It is something we can reach for no matter how dense our neighbourhood or how near our neighbours. In her book *Names for the Sea: Strangers in Iceland,* Sarah Moss relates a tale of a treeless landscape shared by a few farming families in southern Iceland. Although the landscape is vast and its inhabitants few, voices carry. People can be seen across long distances, allowing news to be shared and providing a sense that although there might be miles between one farmer and the next, they are anything but *alone.* They are neighbours: each others' and the land's.

Contrast that with a city with which you are familiar. Have you experienced the sometimes crushing sense of being surrounded by people but able to connect with so few of them? I expect many of us urban-dwellers have. Although loneliness cannot be cured simply by moments of connection with a random assortment of neighbours, realising our interdependence — first in our heads and next in our actions — is a good place to start. Cities are places where we need only look next door to begin.

Sacred Pavement: Neighbourliness

I've kept this chapter short because I think that it defeats the purpose to go on at length about how brilliant a spiritual practice it is to 'be neighbourly' instead of actually doing it. I know firsthand how easy it is to read books on the importance of doing life together with one's neighbours and never step outside the comfort zone...and I'm fairly sociable. The turning point in all this neighbourliness will come for you the moment you put down this book and actually begin relating to the people around you. For me, this was the moment I realised that neighbourliness is not about *niceness* or *politeness* but about nurturing a deep and respectful curiosity for my neighbours. Curiosity takes time and energy and it requires real humility and listening, as do all spiritual practices. There is no guarantee that the neighbours you choose to get to know will extend the same friendliness or curiosity to you. In fact they might resent you for breaking the social norms — but don't let this hold you back. On the other side of the potential awkwardness or suspicion are immensely important friendships to be had, and spiritual steps to be taken.

The Divine is, after all, the great Other; aspects of her face can be glimpsed in all the others we bother getting to know.

As you embark on the adventures below, take some time to reflect, mentally and in your journal, on how the risk of meeting others impacts on your ability to be present to the Divine. How would you hope this would change? What unnerves or excites you about the adventures below?

Urban adventures

1. *Make excuses to meet your neighbours.* You don't need to go knocking door to door. Maybe find a local Residents' Association meeting to attend, or chat to people outside a polling station on an election day. Keep your eyes open for local events or holidays, especially from cultures or traditions different to your own.

2. *Neighbours in fiction.* If you're the sort of person who loves novels, you might find a good book about city-dwellers connecting because of, or even in spite of, their differences. This can be a good way to inspire yourself to pursue the same kind of neighbourliness and connection. A favourite of mine to return to is *The L-Shaped Room* by Lynne Reid Banks. A London boarding house in the 1960s, with all its wonderful variety. Scribble notes in your journal about the characters of whichever novel you choose — what brings them together? Were they able to seek each others' welfare? Do they remind you of any of the people in your life, especially those who live nearby?

3. *X marks my spot.* Spend a week or so gradually sketching a detailed, local map of where you live and what is around you. Are there any neighbours, past or present, whose lives earn a place on that map?

4. *What brings us together.* Another sketch — this time, not a geographical map but a web of connections in your local area. Write down the names of people or community groups in the local area and draw a circle around them. Connect these circles and write the sort of connection on the line in between. For example, between 'Mr Rogers, flat 471' and 'Community hall' you could draw a line that says 'bingo club'. Between 'me' and 'young family in no. 83' you could write, 'we say hello when the kids are on their way to school.'

Do you see any patterns on your map? Any connections it might be easy to strengthen? Any people for whom you feel moved to pray or show kindness toward, or from you'd like to learn?

CHAPTER 6

Neighbours in time

'I guess they sent you here so I could tell you my story,' said Letty, her eyes twinkling behind thick glasses. She picked up her zimmer frame and thumped it back down again as if to emphasise a point she'd made. When I tried to reply, she continued, 'Well, I'm not sure it's much of one.' Never was a statement more falsely humble.

Letty's mostly-deafness makes back-and-forth conversation difficult, but we do our best. On this occasion I tried to remind her that she'd told me her life story twice before, and that I was really here to ask one specific question. I failed. The whole story — or at least the highlights — was coming out again. Caretaking for a crumbling building in the aftermath of World War II whilst raising a passel of children. Working as an advocate for women in the legal and medical systems. The friends who had become letter-writing correspondents in Canada. Being widowed and moving into this care home. Her hopes and fears and ailments.

Letty never stays 'surface level' with her stories; they are woven throughout with her sense of the ups and downs of divine timing, a sense which both comforts and frustrates her. Whenever I am given a glimpse of her story, I am reminded by the layers of personal and communal history that exist in this London we both call home. She knew this city I will never know at a time I will never see, and yet she trusted as I do that a sacred path was there — is still here — to be found and followed amidst the urban rumble and rubble.

Letty's stories, and the stories of many older people whom I meet in my work, stir up in me a deeply local curiosity. As I'm given a glimpse of just one layer of history, I can't help but be interested in how people lived their lives in previous eras. This curiosity extends forward in time, too, and is a significant part of the reason why I choose to live and work in the sphere of spirituality and religion: the question of how *will* people live their lives in the future — materially, spiritually and emotionally? What spiritual resources will be there for future generations, resources which have over time grown richly layered? You don't have to feel a sense of call towards leadership in a particular faith or spiritual community, however, to feel the tug of this curiosity either backwards or forwards in time.

If the previous chapter was about geographical neighbourliness, this chapter is about neighbourliness along another dimension: time. It is about developing a sense of being temporal neighbours with those who have inhabited your city in the past and those who'll inhabit it in the future. Just how different are humans from 100 years ago, and those alive today? Or a thousand years ago? Evolutionary changes in any species don't happen in the blink of an eye. Social, political and spiritual changes, though they may happen at a more accelerated pace today because of our technological capabilities, are neither monolithic nor irreversible. Perhaps a more interesting question for us, as we seek to understand the spiritual importance of connectedness to the pasts of our cities, is: why should the foreignness of the past get in the way of our curiosity about it?

Who among us hasn't played the game of asking, 'If you had a time machine and could visit any time and place, where would it be?' There's a reason for the perpetual popularity of TV shows like *Doctor Who*: the ease with which they allow viewers to play with that thought experiment. In cities, we have countless opportunities to do a bit of imaginative time travel. No time machine needed: just a spot of inquisitiveness and patience. The cultural life of our cities, their historically important places, and the human, oral history held by our neighbours are all fuel for this travel. Delving into these stories, both personal and communal, is something we can engage in as a spiritual practice.

Our urban elders

Through our urban elders, cities can open up to the discerning urban adventurer. Letty is full to bursting with details about her life in this place and the lives she encountered, but sometimes getting to those details is a bit of a labyrinthine task. When I sit down with Letty it can feel like we're involved in some kind of mutual code-breaking: she's trying to get through to me, to be heard and seen, and I am trying to learn something new from her, despite her charming, repetitive forgetfulness. Anyone who has spent time with older relatives and friends can relate to this feeling, both sweet and frustrating at the same time. There's something truly magical about the richness and frailty of memory, and of the delicate alchemy of making spaces for memories to be passed on. Our older neighbours are likely not the reasons we've chosen to live where we do, but they can become our chosen elders: ones whose experience and stories we may choose to hear and whose wisdom we may choose to sit under.

How difficult it can be to actually spend time with older folks in our cities, though. Think about the people you live near, or with whom you work or socialise on a regular basis. Do your daily rhythms of life bring you into meaningful contact with people far older than you? Sometimes urban life becomes so busy that we lose out on the grounding contact with those who are older. And though I don't imagine that everyone reading this book would consider themselves a 'younger person', the sheer speed of urban life can mean we completely bypass those in our midst who don't share that frenetic pace. Pursuing opportunities to meet people outside our age bracket is just that — a pursuit, and one that's potentially richly rewarding.

A few weeks ago, I met a past neighbour. We discovered that we had lived less than 50 yards from each other about eight years ago, in a funny sort-of-cul-de-sac full of 1980s yellow brick houses. He had been there when the houses were built and occupied one ever since; I had been subletting an attic extension three doors down. My former neighbour is a few decades older than me and recently retired from work. We met discussing opportunities for community organising and shared the bittersweet realisation that we'd had the opportunity nearly a decade ago to begin a friendship. Probably because of the difference in our ages and speeds of life, neither of us had taken the time to do so.

Our lives are full of missed opportunities: that is not something to be overly anxious or mournful about, and it's a theme I'll return to in a later chapter. There will always be *could have, should have, would have* moments. Befriending those who are older to you, whose experience of the city has been different, is not about insuring yourself against a sense of 'relational FOMO'.[2] It is about nurturing a spiritual practice, about hopping into the time machine and looking backwards with the help of urban elders. This spiritual practice, I've found, gives rise a concern for those who will come after us. They are the people whose urban elders, or ancestors, we will be.

When it comes to pursuing connections with our urban elders, a lot can obviously go awry. Conflicting points of view, points of irritation and frustration are common across generational differences. Recently, at a training day on working intergenerationally, I was surprised to hear both a number of older colleagues (by 'older' I mean age 60 upwards) and a number of my millennial colleagues both levelling the charge of 'entitlement' at those who were a different generation to them. The older people thought the younger were entitled because they expected opportunities to be handed to them on a platter, and the younger thought the older were entitled because they expected automatic respect and power because of having lived longer. Simply by airing these perceptions about age, experience and entitlement we were able to have a remarkably constructive conversation on where the sources of respect, power and opportunity are in our work and our communities.

---

[2] That's 'Fear of missing out' for those of you who have the good sense not to use internet lingo in everyday speech!

You may not work in and amongst communities in all their messy glory, nor with people with a great age diversity. It's still worth taking stock of your assumptions about people older and younger than you as you embark on the Urban Adventures of getting to know them and their spiritual experiences. What do you assume people of a different age to you will value? Will want to talk about? Will reflect on as most important? Fundamentally, where do these assumptions come from? Take a moment and think, journal, even sketch through some of these questions. We'll return to them in the Adventures below.

The unphotographed ones

Every so often I'll catch sight of some old photographs from the early twentieth century that were originally black-and-white but have been colorized. Despite my great love for monochrome photography, the moment in which color is added to old photographs never fails to catch me off-guard in the best way. The vivacity of these photos leaps out at me through their slightly garish colours, a reminder that those who lived in the past didn't live it in monochrome. Experiences like this stir my curiosity for the unphotographed pasts — the histories to which our access is limited to books, sculpture and paintings, those forms of art requiring us to use more of our imagination because they are less exact.

So far in this chapter, I've been encouraging you to seek connection with your older neighbours and with older traditions, institutions and patterns, so that you might get a deeper sense of the spiritual pulses of your city. But what about the unphotographed ones, the neighbours who've long been pushing up daisies, and the pasts we can't discover over a shared cup of coffee? Those are our urban ancestors rather than elders, and though the connection over time is more tenuous, their spiritual importance is not necessarily lessened because of it.

How then are we to approach our neighbours in time and develop our intergenerational curiosity even further? In this task the many faith traditions of our world become helpful, with their varying concepts of what it means to keep fellowship with those who have lived before us. Some belief systems speak of past lives — of knowing ourselves as having existed in cultures, eras and locations completely foreign to us now but somehow, familiar to us in our very bones. Others speak of a partnership with or reverence for our neighbours in the near or distant past, referring to them as ancestors or saints with which we can be in communion, or ascended masters who still impart wisdom. These unphotographed folks have made and still make a contribution to the world. No matter the metaphysics, we can draw from their lives endless inspiration and challenge.

A sense of humanity's interconnectedness over time is no less crucial now than it has ever been. I write this not only because of the discomfiting experience that many of us have had of feeling rootless when it comes to faith, spirituality, or culture; but also because of how our links with the past inevitably affect how we live now, and how we relate to those who'll come after us. Looking back nudges us also to look forward. What world do we wish to pass on to future generations, physically and spiritually?

Urban dwellers who wish to take their spirituality seriously will find themselves reckoning with this dual curiosity about past and future generations. Why? Because of the speed with which change comes to our urban environments: change which is wrought in large part by humans. Our cities are very plastic, susceptible to constant change. Urban spirituality is at least in part about learning how to navigate constant change, inside and out. What are the things, whose are the stories, which are the practices which give us spiritual anchors amidst the whirl of change? And which helps us to negotiate when we are undergoing change within ourselves?

One potential pitfall of looking back at our neighbours in time is the pleasant yet problematic phenomenon of nostalgia. Defined as a 'sentimental, wistful longing for a past time,' nostalgia's rose-tinted spectacles are always tempting to put on. If we look at those who have come before us only through a nostalgic lens, romanticising their lives and experiences, or only choosing to hear about the good in their 'good old days', then we are likely to look towards the future a bit unprepared for when hard times may come. What's more, we can get in the rut of thinking, 'If only things were simple, like they were back then...'

Life has never been simple, not even for pre-human hunter-gatherer ancestors. Nostalgia for a golden past makes us irresponsible in the present and careless for the future. If current environmental crises are anything to go by, it is ever more important that we realise our ability to shape our physical and spiritual 'now' and 'not yet'. Here in the UK I've come across an interesting illustration of this point from the natural world in the work of Merlin Sheldrake, a scientist who specialises in fungi. His work deals with the ways in which the 'roots' of mushrooms — which have the rather fantastic name of *mycorrhizae* — form vast networks across the forest and are able to exchange energy, nutrients and even what can legitimately be called messages across huge distances. Who knew mushrooms 'talk' to one another? Sheldrake calls this network the 'Wood-Wide Web'.

On one level, this is just a fascinating natural occurrence. However, I see it also as a spiritual picture of what it's like to be human. We are never completely autonomous but rather connected to the rest of one single human network over time. We can dig deep into what our species' wood-wide web has to offer, which are the spiritual resources for life. There's not much room for nostalgia here (it doesn't really serve anyone); there's just care for life, smarts for survival and even moments of breathtaking insight or beauty. We might not be able to comprehend the lives of the billions of humans who've shared this planet, but that doesn't mean that their contributions to the wood-wide web are lost.

What if your city is small and young?

Their density of population and speed of change make cities excellent places to hone your curiosity and humility in relation to the past, as well as your sense of connection to the human wood-wide web. It doesn't matter whether you live in a huge metropolis or a medium-sized town — both are great places to dig deep. The nearest city to where I grew up in rural Michigan was less than 200 years old. Like so many white Americans and Australians, my perception of time and the ages of things was a bit more truncated than many Asians, Africans and Europeans, who've lived amongst ancient history all their lives. I still remember my first encounter with something from the Roman Era in Britain and the awe I felt. That this bit of wall from ancient Londonium should just be casually sitting around in the shadow of modern skyscrapers still fries my brain a bit!

Let me say it plainly, though: you don't have to live in a city that's 3000 years old or has a population of 2 million souls in order to cultivate curiosity. If anything, living in a place with a smaller size and less history is a tantalising reminder that there is more out there, older cities, different stories, unfamiliar and fascinating ways of being human. Digging deep into what is a part of your city's human past often leaves you with an appetite for more, and that's no bad thing.

What if you turn up difficult stuff?

Inevitably, when you go digging into the human past of a city, your metaphorical shovel is going to turn up some difficult debris. We are humans, after all, bundles of light and dark, choices made that have brought wholeness and some that have brought harm. To be spiritually open, leading with your spiritual senses of empathy, stillness and imagination, is to be in a fairly vulnerable state, which is why I warn you now.

Some years ago I was lucky enough to be invited to visit Cape Town on behalf of the institution where I was working and training. Half business trip and half holiday, I embarked on this journey with an incredible amount of openness and empathy. We didn't remain solely in the business and tourist districts, but on a couple of occasions visited contacts in some of the township communities located beyond Cape Town itself.

Gugulethu, Nyanga, Khayelitsha: the names were new on my tongue and the harshness of life was evident, even if I knew what to expect from a shantytown. Meeting locals, sharing delicious meat straight off the braai, and going to one of my favourite church services ever, it was truly a culture shock to get in our car and drive back into the prosperous city centre. Back there, we were able to give some more context to our experiences in the townships by visiting the District Six Museum, which documents in painstaking human detail the expulsion of the black and 'coloured' (South African slang for mixed-race) people from central Cape Town during the Apartheid.

The cruel reality of Apartheid may officially be past, but it is clear that for large sections of Cape Town and South Africa's population generally, especially those who live in the townships, Apartheid has a long echo. For most of the trip I was silent — something which almost never happens for this extrovert — seeing and processing and being a little in shock at times, even as I could see the goodness, creativity and beauty in Cape Town alongside the injustice. For weeks after, I was unsettled in spirit by what I had seen and learned, and angry that I had spent some decades of my life not quite realising what the segregation had meant and what it still cost the people of South Africa.

I share this story because it was a moment in my life which brought home to me again the cost of being spiritually open to our neighbours in time, to the realities of traumas past, to learn about the past with your spiritual and emotional senses to the fore, not just your intellect. Although Cape Town may be geographically distant from anywhere I ever settle, the interconnectedness of humanity — our wood-wide web —

means that we are never far from the more difficult aspects of our history as a species, especially in an increasingly globalised age. In the next chapter, I'll delve deeper in how to work with the challenging things that can come up when you pursue spiritual development in urban spaces, both how you can prepare well and also care well for yourself and others when this occurs.

Sacred Pavement: Neighbours in time

Allowing the pasts of our cities to be a guide to us contains both risk and reward. In the past we encounter the messiness of being human, the messiness of all life, whether urban or rural. The great gift of doing this work intentionally and in a city is how we really can't ever forget that we aren't alone in the mess. The sheer number of people, layers of history, varieties of experience of that history is what keeps this reminder active. Though it may seem overly simple, even a cliché, the realisation of our ultimate identity as beings connected over time, unique but not alone, is worth a great deal. We are invited to expand our empathy and learn how to show reverence to those who've lived before us. As we do this adventuring and as we consider what kind of ancestors we will be for those who come after, our living urban elders, along with the 'unphotographed ones', have got our backs.

Urban Adventures

1. *Layers of your own history.* A good way of slowing down and beginning to develop a patience for human history is to look at your own history/herstory in microcosm. Try cultivating a curiosity for just a day's worth of your own history. By sketching or writing, visually represent what one day in your recent life has held. If you already have a detailed reflective journaling practice, switch it up, and use a different means of recording your experiences. Mind-map instead of draw, or draw instead of write.

2. *The Examen.* You can develop this personal reflection from no. 1 further by adapting a Jesuit practice called the Examen, or examination of consciousness. This is not unlike the game that some children play around the dinner table with a parent called 'Highs and Lows', where everyone has to share a high and low point of their day. The Examen goes deeper, and asks the questions: where have you felt most alive and energised during the day, and where have you felt most depleted and least like yourself? In the former, you can detect where you've been most aligned with the Spirit, and in the latter where you've been most out of alignment.

3. *Urban elders.* Find an opportunity to connect with those older than you — no matter what age you are. Do you have older neighbours? Are there older colleagues in your workplace you could have lunch with? Is there a care home or day centre where you could volunteer? Pursue a

meaningful conversation with someone whose experience of the city has predated yours. Perhaps ask a person or two if they might write or draw something you can paste in your journal. How has their faith or spirituality been shaped by life in this city? What has it taught them? What didn't they expect about this journey?

4. *Groups holding history.* There is a lot of good material out there about habit forming and morning rituals, so much to explore in terms of do-it-yourself rituals, some of which you probably already practice! That's great. But often, rituals are developed to hold us as communal beings. Your task here is one of an anthropologist: to observe three different faith or spiritual groups' rituals, and partake only as far as you feel able. What is the ritual marking, or remembering in the actions and bodies of those present? What felt easeful about the ritual, and did anything feel forced? If you can, ask someone from the group what spirituality or prayer means for them.

In your journal, record that ritual in as much detail as you can as soon after the experience as possible, writing and drawing cues for yourself. Map the movement, the materials and the meanings you could infer. Leave that journal entry alone for a few days, and then return to it with more distance. What strikes you about what you wrote & how you experienced that example of meaning-making? What has happened to your sense of connection to these faith groups?

CHAPTER 7

Seeking the hidden

There's a mediaeval tradition in mapmaking which is about as macro as macro can get. Enthusiastic and confident cartographers during the middle ages, often working in cooperation with a church, would sometimes be commissioned to create a *mappa mundi* — an entire-world map. These were not the rectangular projections most of us encountered in school, with longitudes, latitudes and tidy political boundaries. They were a more creative form of mapmaking, sometimes depicting the world as a giant chubby body, often that of a divine figure, usually Christ. Instead of anatomical parts and organs, there would be islands, continents, forests, rivers, towns and even fantastical creatures. Places which the cartographers deemed most important were given central location: the world of this map literally revolved around them.

Mappa mundis were a profoundly spiritual endeavour, imbuing the physical world with the imagination and the faith perspective of the maps' artists and commissioners. So much of what you are doing as you work your way through this book is similar work, which is joining up the physical, the spiritual and the imaginative. I've encouraged you to see your spiritual urban journey as a form of mapmaking of the soul, mapping both your city and your journey within it. In any map — medieval or contemporary, physical or spiritual — there will be some areas marked 'here be dragons.' There will be places that over time have become hidden, places which fall off the edges for some reason, or are forced there. We're going to spend some time with these hidden or abandoned places in this chapter.

Kopfkino in Berlin

It took a while, during my first visit to Berlin, for me to realise how this polished city just barely hides its enticingly layered and at times lawless past. The penny began to drop on the day we spent wandering downtown, visiting the Höfe, the little open-air courtyards, in central Berlin. One of them in particular still looked like I imagine Berlin must have looked in the early 90s just after the Wall came down. Bars, live music, tiny galleries, even a few rooms which proclaimed themselves to be the Museum of Contemporary Trash Art. Without realising what I'd been missing, wandering into the Hof at Rosenthalerstraße 39 had transported me some way back in time.

On leaving the Hof, it felt as if the effects of that time travel took a while to wear off. I had peeked beneath the surface and glimpsed Berlin as it had been known not so long ago: a Berlin that was a bit chaotic and patched up, Poor But Sexy, rather than the flashy Berlin The 21st Century Global Metropolis, which brand other parts of the city seemed to be trying hard to sell to me. Suddenly I was able to use both my eyes and my imagination to spot the vestiges of a city still recovering from the extraordinary events of the last century, some of those events playing out in my mind's eye.

A few days after this discovery, my then-boyfriend and I were out walking in Mitte, the neighbourhood where he'd lived during his student days. We were wandering aimlessly, popping into galleries, shops and cafes, when a gated entrance to another Hof caught our eyes. It was open, unusually, the courtyards behind it empty and light, without delivery trucks or other shop doors. Obviously, we had to check it out.

The further we got into the network of courtyards, the more I was convinced I must be trespassing. My partner assured me that Berlin was still a relaxed place: if we were trespassing, we'd be firmly asked to leave but nothing worse. (This did nothing to assuage my American hyperawareness about private property.) But no grumpy security guard materialised, and finally we emerged in a large open yard surrounding a tall, derelict building with several stories of windows, with what looked like a covered porch attached. Directly over a wrought iron fence to the south stood the vast, gorgeous, triple-cupola New Synagogue which faces Oranienburger Straße. Here at the Synagogue's back we found what appeared to have been part of a Jewish hospital — investigating signs and peering in windows provided enough evidence for us to come to this conclusion . We tried doors and gates, aiming to get in, but all was clearly sealed up and signed with warnings not to enter the deteriorating structure. Eventually we gave up, making our way back out to the street rather than hop some more fences and get caught around the back of the Synagogue.

As we walked out my partner asked what I was thinking. I confessed that in my head I was pretending to be a spy on the escape, trying to get out onto the street where I could get lost in a crowd of people with whatever secret microfilm I had picked up at the abandoned hospital. He laughed and said that in Berlin it was easy to get caught up in *kopfkino* ('head-cinema' — what a brilliant German word!) when confronted with the surprises of the past which are hidden in plain sight. My playful imagination aside, our little adventure ended as it had started: without any drama. Back on the street I felt the same way as I had at Rosenthalerstraße 39 — not quite fully back in the present.

On a separate visit to Berlin, I came into contact with another of its ramshackle wonders, the Tempelhofer Feld. It is a ruin of a socialist-era airport smack dab in central Berlin. The terminal of Tempelhof hosts occasional tours, but mostly it lies empty and quiet, the vast concrete network of runways stretching away from it to the south and east. I took the underground train to Paradenstraße and alighted, walking around the terminal in a kind of hushed trance. The September day was sunny and breezy, and some old flagpoles without flags were clanking in the wind. The noise echoed around the boomerang-curve of the terminal in a way that was less eerie than tentative. I couldn't see a good way to climb in, so I abandoned my urbex plan set off across the Feld instead.

It only takes about 40 minutes to cross but I took much longer, stopping to people-watch. A group of young hipsters on rollerblade-and-windsurfing contraptions rode the breeze across the concrete runways, avoiding strips of grass. Groups of children with their foreign au pairs traipsed alongside me, less impressed than I at the few ruined airplanes rusting away on the north edge of the Feld. Benches made from reclaimed wood pallets had been dotted here and there, and I stopped at several to sit and look. Occasionally I came across a burnt spot where a bonfire or fireworks had clearly been set alight. On the east side, a collection of tidily chaotic allotments were nestled close enough to the gentrifying neighbourhood of Neukölln for easy tending. In Neukölln I re-entered the noise of the city, feeling oddly famished with hunger. Luckily a record shop-café served a bowl of hummus and bread as big as my head — a welcome grounding after the spacey hours I'd spent crossing the crumbling runways.

The downtown Höfe — the Jewish hospital — the Tempelhof airport. Why do I tell you all these stories, just a few of the times I've felt I'm somehow dipped into a dream, participating in something of Berlin's identity which lies beneath the surface? It's because experiences like these are more than just learning about a city's hidden past, if we allow them to be. As I've been saying repeatedly throughout this book, our urban environments can lend beautiful shape to our inner environments, our inner lives. Encountering the less-polished, the hidden, and the abandoned in our cities, we may gain strength to encounter that in us and in our relationship to the Divine which is less-polished, hidden or abandoned. Sometimes we may encounter things which challenge or frighten us: this is part of the adventure. A healthy and maturing spirituality is one that doesn't shy away from these encounters, and knows the importance of spaces of safety and belovedness alongside them.

In this chapter we'll look at three aspects of seeking the hidden: the abandoned, the underground, and that which is 'hidden' in history. Before we launch in, I'd like to reiterate how important it is for you, as an urban adventurer, to have places and practices of safety and grounding set up before you start deliberately exploring these hidden things, because of what they have the potential to provoke. Take a moment here to pause with your journal, to sketch or write for a while about how you come back to yourself, to the present moment, to a sense of the goodness of the Spirit, when you encounter something which unsettles you. Do you have a physical posture, breathing pattern, short prayer or affirmation? From time to time I use one or all of these things when my urban, spiritual adventures turn up something challenging for me.

Abandoned spaces

It was only after marrying my German boyfriend and beginning the adventure of encountering Berlin as not just a tourist destination, but as my capital-in-law, that I really began to reckon with the experiences like the ones I related above. As an American I'd always had a rather different relationship to abandoned buildings or places, almost all of which I'd encountered having been rural ones. An abandoned 70-year-old gas station has a different feel, needless to say, than an abandoned Belle Époque cultural centre or Cold War era listening station.

I realised that my fascination with abandoned spaces had to do with their spiritual meaning as well as their aesthetics. Abandoned spaces are hidden in plain sight, often not actually that difficult to find, though sometimes difficult to enter. They beg of curious visitors a set of obvious questions: why was this place important to people, and why did it cease to be so? What is still here that no one felt worth taking with them, or couldn't take with them? Why is this place still not in use? In these empty places there's ample room and quiet. We can listen to our own inner narratives about use and disuse, ease and unease. They have a magnifying effect on our inner lives, but not only that. Unlike explicitly religious spaces — which have a similar effect — these spaces are uncared for, in between one purpose and the next. They are liminal and as such draw out what's liminal in us, the things which don't quite fit in one place, one aspect of our being, or another.

In London, my current home, urban space is at a premium and as such abandoned spaces are harder and harder to find. Within the last 18 months, the newspapers were telling of planning permission given to 200 new skyscraper-height buildings across the city, naturally to mixed reactions. Besides this construction, the 'filling in' of green spaces or edges of parkland, empty lots, and previously derelict post-industrial spaces is common. We haven't quite reached the same situation as in New York City, where pencil-thin buildings are built ever taller, their developers having acquired the rights of the 'unused airspace' of the adjacent city blocks. These are just two cities, both in the West; the skylines of Mumbai, Singapore, Dubai, Tokyo and Shanghai are also growing cluttered with glass and metal. What does it mean in this age of urban crowding to seek out what's abandoned?

In one way, to seek out abandoned urban spaces as a spiritual practice is to insist on the value and virtue of the empty, the melancholy and the ambiguous. This isn't a new insistence, but it's one that continues to be important. There are so many spiritual narratives around, both from outside and inside of established faith traditions, which devalue anything which is difficult or confusing about the spiritual life. The less-than-sunny parts of our lives are no less spiritually important, no less formative for us. Abandoned urban spaces especially get us asking about those parts in us, becoming gently curious about our own shadows.

Seeking abandoned spaces as a spiritual practice also introduces an ecological perspective.

Making mini-pilgrimages to abandoned spaces, it's hard to ignore how many of them are slowly (or not so slowly) being reclaimed by the natural world. Grass sprouts up between slabs of concrete. Tree branches invade empty window frames. Moss, lichen and ivy run riot over previously manicured trellises, yards and walls. In cities, where humans often work hard to keep nature at bay, abandoned corners become oases of unruly green, explosions of leafy chaos.

I find a bright and unabashed hope in the tenacity of nature to survive that which humanity builds to subdue it. In the times we inhabit, the human race is realising how we must come to terms with what our actions do to this gorgeous planet. We are learning — sometimes slowly and unevenly — to find ways of living more in cooperation with the earth rather than by taking advantage of it. To witness abandoned spaces being reclaimed by nature, then, is an act of witness. We witness the 'comeback', the wisdom of life beyond our own species. In our day and age this is a source of crucial encouragement and challenge.

Director Alex Garland's film *Annihilation* from 2018 is a brilliant meditation on exactly some of these themes. In the film, a play on the alien invasion genre, a group of scientists explore abandoned areas of Florida swampland, investigating an unknown alien life form with abilities to mimic and mutate the patterns and bodies of earth-bound creatures, including humans. The dreamlike script takes viewers through stages of curiosity, horror, confusion and ultimately respect for the natural world, as the alien life form tries to gain the upper hand. Viewers are left with questions about whether humans behave more like an 'invasive species' than any trope-y alien ever could.

In urban areas, these questions are always alive. For city dwellers the possibility of living well and in cooperation with nature presents itself to us in the ordinary places of slippage between human creation and natural reclamation: a disused parking lot, abandoned buildings, post-industrial sites. A temptation exists, however, when encountering abandoned urban spaces, to treat them with the same shallow consumerism as we might treat a beautiful mountain vista. There is a reason that 'nature is healing' has become a meme. The phrase or hashtag 'ruin porn' occasionally makes the rounds in thinkpieces, rightfully criticising the instagram-isation of the Urban Exploration movement, the unchallenged nostalgia it can create, the glorification of wastefulness. These things are just as problematic as the 'spirituality stock photo' issue. In the pursuit of the spiritual medicine of abandoned places, how easily we fall into the trap of commodifying them.

The clue to avoiding the pitfalls of commodification and ruin porn is in what we take away from our experience of these spaces. I used the word *medicine* just now to talk about the benefits we might receive, and this word is crucial. Medicine is not nourishment: medicine addresses a problem. We take it when we are experiencing ailments, not when we're healthy. The medicine of abandoned urban spaces, especially those being visibly re-inhabited by nature, addresses the illness of human over-expansion. It addresses our dis-ease and fears about our relationship to non-human creatures. It addresses our over-dependence on disposable things and non-renewable energy. These illnesses are as spiritual as they are social.

Before you go about exploring abandoned spaces, spend some time in conversation and reflection on which of these issues, and others, you need medicine to address. After your explorations, it's up to you to ask yourself if the medicine has worked. What changes have begun within you as a result and what might you do differently going forward? We'll return to these and other questions below in the Urban Adventure, and the next chapter on 'Finding stubborn nature' will expand further on this topic.

There's a world going on underground

While this book was in its first draft, the brilliant nature writer Robert Macfarlane, long a favorite of mine, published his latest tome, *Underland*. Macfarlane is a master of rich, descriptive prose. He goes beyond simply anthropomorphising the landscape and, subtly, does the opposite: he gives a land-ly shape to our human lives and patterns. When it comes to the urban landscape, Macfarlane has written in *Edgelands* about those spaces where city gives way to country, not in quite the same way as the abandoned spaces I wrote about above, but with a similar feel. I bring up Macfarlane not only to celebrate his work, which is excellent, but to point out how in a sense he has been working up (or working down) to *Underland* for years, in all his writing about mountaineering, marginal spaces, nature walks and vocabulary.

Underground spaces tug at us in a way that is difficult to describe. In cities, the accumulated materials of human life over the centuries mean that street levels get higher and higher over the years, creating a kind of 'overground underground' of previous layers of human history. In London, you can visit a Mithraeum, a temple to the god Mithras, that dates from Roman times. In order to visit, you must enter a tediously generic office block and descend seven metres to a quiet, dimly lit exhibition space. From there you are admitted a dozen at a time to the ruins, which lie at where ground level would have been in Roman Londinium. The ruins are fairly simple, and don't give away much detail about the all-male mystery cult of Mithras.

In Rome, a more extant Mithraeum lies beneath the church of San Clemente in Laterano. My favourite church in Rome (so far, I've only visited the city once and one visit is not enough to see all the churches!), San Clemente is an urban adventure par excellence. On entering the 11th-century church through a rather humble little porch you're greeted by a stunning mosaic on the east wall, a garden of paradise with the Tree of Life flowering. It's a vision of life in all its trajectory of fullness as imagined by the earliest Christian communities. Once you can bear to leave this magnificent sight, you turn off into one of the aisles, walking down a flight or two of stairs to enter the first subterranean level. This is another church, dating from at least the 4th century CE. There is little remaining except a vast space, with rows of columns and quiet alcoves. This space had been built to incorporate the house of a Roman gentleman who had originally hosted the church in his home.[3]

Beneath all this, the street level during the 4th century, is another layer, again going further back into the Roman era to the 2nd century CE. Here are ruins of several Roman dwellings as well as the alleys and streets between them, and a larger space which served for a time as a Mithraeum. It's a smaller space to the one in London but has more archaeological goodies — but still not enough to give a strong picture of what the Mithraists got up to on a regular basis. Eating, mostly, maybe after a ritual bull sacrifice. Maybe singing? Definitely going to the toilet.

On the album 'Swordfishtrombones', Tom Waits sings, *'There's a world going on underground.'* This lyric always comes to my mind when considering urban subterranean spaces, except I'd probably say that there are *worlds*, plural, rather than just one. Visiting the Mithraea of London, Rome, and elsewhere, I've been plunged into some of these ancient underground worlds. These spaces aren't so much deliberately hidden or abandoned as they are partially forgotten. Street levels moved up and culture moved on.

As with abandoned spaces, going underground brings out that which we might usually try to keep hidden. We as a species didn't need to wait for the development of psychology as a doctrine in the 18th and 19th centuries to know about the richness of the subconscious, though we might have used different words for it. Religions worldwide, living, dormant, and extinct, have cherished legends of holy caves in which divine

---

[3] The original graves of Saints Cyril and Methodius are there, which I discovered to my delight. The inventors of the precursor to the Cyrillic alphabet, unfortunately, have to share a feast day with St Valentine, Feb 14th, so they get frequently overlooked. Sorry, guys.

encounters, transformations, or other significant events took place.[4] In urban spaces, our caves are not filled with stalactites, but there are still tunnels and columns, underground aquifers, graffiti and echoey chambers.

For me, going underground in a city as a spiritual practice is a counterpoise: I use it to balance out the theme in my spirituality about God / the divine being present above, over and beyond us. Many cosmologies and holy texts picture the Divine as distant and above, with angelic beings of the 'higher realms' to heed, and 'ascension' as a worthy pursuit. I don't necessarily dispute these cosmologies — in fact, I find the idea of the utter beyond-ness of the divine to be helpful and true. However, it is not the whole story: God is also to be found beneath our feet. We need both Divine immanence *and* transcendence.

Going underground, our senses pick up changes: the muffled noise, reduced (or absent) light, strange smells and changed temperatures. Although there are worlds going on down there, they don't jostle in the same way. To go underground is to retreat awhile from the world above and the pressures of the day. This deliberate *hiding* that is natural to underground spaces is what takes the experience from being simply a sensory one to one that is sensual. By this I mean not just perceiving with the senses but through the senses experiencing an intimacy: an intimacy with the divine.

Dedicated practitioners of this intimacy, the Desert Mothers and Fathers, Christian mystics of the early centuries CE, urged their followers to 'Go into the cave of your heart' and 'Go to your

[4] One of my favourite of these is the legend of the Shinto goddess Ameratsu, whose refuge-taking in a cave deprives the whole earth of light. She has to be enticed out of the cave by a bunch of raving deities — raving in the sense of having a dance party in the dark.

cell; your cell will teach you everything.' They weren't the only ones; an instruction to retreat to a place of aloneness, burrowing into the cave at the core of one's being, is an ancient practice common to many spiritual traditions. The Desert Mothers and Fathers certainly would not have imagined or recommended doing so in urban areas, but for us city-dwellers with little access to literal deserts, their injunctions still hold value for us. Going underground in urban areas is a way of furnishing the caves of our hearts with stillness, so that we might be able to return to that stillness when we can't physically visit an underground space, or any place that has a spiritual meaning for us.

Does the idea of furnishing a cave sound silly? Perhaps it is. Then again, there's a lot in the spiritual life which is about getting over our tendencies to take everything so seriously, to get over ourselves a bit, to stay *down to earth*. To experience the quirkiness of life with a playful levity makes space for the Spirit to breathe with and through us, and not just to breathe, but to laugh. Going underground literally or metaphorically doesn't have to equal being sombre or melancholy. Sometimes it's about discovering the ingenuity, humour, and joy of previous generations.

In the British Museum there's a brilliant example of how underground spaces keep things light. The rooms dedicated to ancient Assyria contain twin stone statues, once flanking the entrance to the temple and palace of King Ashurnasirpal II. Excavated from what is today part of Iraq and brought to the Museum, these once-buried gates each contain a forbidding sculpture of a human-headed lion, easily more than twice the height of a person. Around the side of one of the statues, however, a much less forbidding treasure awaits. Now covered by a bit of plexiglass to protect it, you can see where someone has carved lines into the stone in order to play a simple game, an ancient version of tic-tac-toe.[5] When I first discovered this I was in stitches with laughter, imagining the fearsome, bearded palace guards of one of the most bombastic leaders of the ancient world, getting royally bored with their shifts at the gates and scratching a game into the stone so they could pass the long hours on watch. Did King Ashurnasirpal ever find out? How many pairs of guards used the game-board to keep awake?

People get up to all sorts of nonsense, don't we, when we think we're not being watched. I don't mean stuff that is sinister — I mean stuff that's odd, embarrassing, and funny. Whether ancient board games, or the ubiquitous rude graffiti of any age (of which the British Museum also has a great collection), the earthiness and humour of it all to be celebrated. That which is forgotten or hidden about human life is not always fearful. Both the Mithraea and the Assyrian gates were for some eras lost completely to view, buried underground, then lately rediscovered. What have they hidden below the surface? Mysterious religious observance and the trappings of empire, yes, but also humour and brotherhood, the ingenuity and intimacy of everyday life thousands of years ago.

Seeking out the womb-like underground spaces of a city as a spiritual practice helps me to remember and practice my prayer *in the nearness of God*, without being embarrassed by my own foibles — by the quirky furnishings of my own cave, as the mystics would say. Cities offer us subterranean spaces where

---

[5] For my UK readers — tic-tac-toe is what you call 'noughts and crosses.'

we find what's been forgotten, the serious as well as the silly. Although in the next section we'll tackle the difficult things, it's important to remember that not all we find in the shadows is fearful or bleak.

What history would rather forget

The Mithraeum in London is not actually in its original location. Roman Londinium's Mithraeum was quite a ways further down Walbrook towards Watling Street — two streets which still exist today, more or less near the now-subterranean river and Roman road from which they get their names. Why was the Mithraeum moved? In short, because no one knew about it before 1954, when post-World War II rebuilding around the City of London unearthed it beneath a planned office building redevelopment. To make space for this and other developments, the Mithraeum was relocated to an open air space at street level in the 1960s. It wasn't until the early 2000s when further developments and disputes over ownership resulted in another relocation of the ruins, fairly close to their original location, this time bringing them back down to Roman ground level.

Had it not been for the Blitz, during which much of the City of London had been flattened by bombs, the 1954 redevelopments may never have unearthed the Mithraeum. Stories of architectural discoveries like this crop up all over southern England where the bombs fell, including a Roman complex in Canterbury, for example. The violent outbursts of the twentieth century have given access to many a hidden, long-inaccessible space. Coming into contact with these spaces, we can't ignore that the history which has hidden or unearthed them is soaked in that which is worst about humanity: violence, oppression, cruelty and war. What are we to make of the juxtaposition of these things with the spiritual importance of hidden and abandoned spaces?

From my location in England, it is easy and common to spot vilification of the Germans for their roles in twentieth century atrocities. But it is not only the German people who have a particular duty towards exhuming and laying to rest that which is not so much hidden but rather wilfully abandoned to history. Both British and American attitudes towards empire or manifest destiny, for example, are too often excused or ignored. Human history is rife with examples of power used badly, and these examples aren't limited to the West. We've got to wrestle, spiritually, with this reality, especially as we come across it frequently in our encounters with hidden urban spaces.

In my journey towards priesthood, I've had a hell of a lot to reckon with in my own faith tradition. As a woman, a queer person, an inquisitive doubter, and a hybrid in many ways, staying with the faith I'd accepted as a child and stepping up as a leader within it was not the most straightforward route in life for me to take. I had to excavate my faith in order to re-inhabit it, or else leave it behind. I learned how to be healthily suspicious with people like Phyllis Trible, to identify particular 'texts of terror' in the context of spiritual history: both literal texts as well as historical occurrences. From Itumelong Mosala I learned to treat texts and histories and traditions as 'sites of struggle', in which the pursuit of justice and peace for all took place, and still takes place.

I tell you this snippet of my own journey in order to help

you frame how you encounter the 'texts' or locations of terror you might encounter when you go digging in your Urban Adventures. Terror is a strong word, but often not too strong for what we find in hidden, abandoned or subterranean spaces. Take another example from Berlin: this one, a good example of how a text of terror has become a site of struggle, an urban space has preserved something that history might be tempted to hide. Near the Brandenburg Gate is an area (roughly a city block's worth) which stands in memorial to the Holocaust. It is maze-like, with short, raised rectangular structures giving way to tall columns, within and around which visitors can wander. When I first visited I had never been to a Jewish graveyard before, so I did not spot the resonance with the raised tombs.

This highly desirable large area in central Berlin is set aside, not for entertainment or financial gain or luxury housing flats but for a memorial. This is astounding to me for what it says about our urban spaces' spiritual significance. Here, something that might have been hidden is in full view; something truly horrific, something which must not be forgotten lest it be repeated. Here there is a reminder in concrete slabs that history — as it is lived out every day — is a site of struggle for peace and justice.

Sacred Pavement: Seeking the hidden

As you delve into the history and hidden parts of your city and cities around the world, you will encounter difficult things. These shadow sides of your city and yourself will inevitably become more present, or more perceptible, as you explore the abandoned and subterranean spaces around you. Rather than fearing or avoiding these shadows, I'd invite you simply to make sure you have patterns and people in place to support you when they appear. Patterns like journaling, moving your body, and making creative work in response to what you encounter. These things provide comfort but also help us process what we find, rather than immediately try to flee it. People offer support and wisdom in the form of a listening ear, and an outsider perspective. Hidden or abandoned spaces offer a specific medicine to us, as I've written above. Trusted people give us space to reflect on where and what types of medicine might be needed in our lives, and what effects it might have in how we live. The people who help us form healthy patterns and receive our medicine might be friends, therapists, mentors, spiritual directors, wise people in our faith communities, family members, or connections we've made elsewhere.

The shadows we encounter in this urban, spiritual work can't be avoided — and in fact it's a losing game trying to ignore or repress them. The more complicated and life-giving work is in recognising their existence alongside the more easeful aspects of our lives and the lives of our cities. With the right patterns and people alongside you, helping you navigate the ever-intertwined in abandoned and underground urban landscapes, you have nothing to fear.

Urban Adventures

1. *Who are the people who help you receive your medicine?* Those you can reflect with on your spiritual journey, either because they're in a similar place to you, or have gleaned wisdom you'd like to access? And what are the rhythms or practices you have in place for processing what you find? Do you know what thing could be particularly triggering for you? Make a list of these people, these practices, these potential triggers in your journal.

2. *Abandoned spaces.* If you can't think of any of these in your city off the top of your head, have a quick web search, or stop in a brick-and-mortar bookshop and ask what they have on hand. Plan a trip to one or two nearby, and document the trip in your journal by mapping your route and the site itself. You can even turn it into a treasure map, documenting what you find.

3. *Underground spaces.* This is a similar task to no. 2, except to focus on underground spaces, not necessarily abandoned. Cellars, foot tunnels, storage areas, etc. Bring a bit of writing with you which you like, a paragraph or a poem. Read it aloud, and take a recording of the sound. Try recording just the ambient sounds — you can play these back at a later date, perhaps as white noise the next time you meditate.

4. *Hidden in history.* In searching out the abandoned and underground spaces in your city, you'll probably have come across some of the things which have been hidden in the

history of that place. Have any of them surprised, unsettled, or moved you? Use these as prompts for creative writing or sketching.

5. *Historic maps.* Go to a bookshop or a library in search of old maps of your city from previous decades or centuries. Copy some of these into your journal, and see if you can find a trace of where your current life, and routes would have been in the past.

6. *Mappa mundi.* Create your own mappa mundi. Depict the whole of your 'known world' in whatever way makes most sense to you, drawing in the features both real and imaginary which give shape to that landscape.

CHAPTER 8

Finding stubborn nature

Currently I am at war with a fox. What an awful thing to write, no? For all my lines and lines about ecological crisis and respect for non-human life, here I am, thinking murderous, American-gun-happy thoughts about the sometime inhabitants of my garden. City foxes are bold, mangy things — no respecters of vegetable patches, constantly leaving rubbish around and making you very aware of their, erm, nocturnal sexytimes. I could just about bear the screeching but there's something about the constant destruction of a garden which just doesn't endear me to them.

The urban fox has a long and conflicted lineage in Britain, never really having been ousted from the cities after the industrial revolution in the 19th century. My neighbourhood, one that has 'Green' in the name, is not a very green place any longer, but it bears ghostly marks of the countryside it occupied not too long ago. During the long and slow rebuilding of London after the Blitz, urban wildlife populations skyrocketed. Former bomb sites and post-industrial 'edgelands' were havens for all sorts of animals.[6] My favourite local urban legend tells the story of postwar no-go-zone in my part of town, one which was

---

[6] *Edgelands* is another word I owe to a book by Robert Macfarlane.

dangerous not because of bomb rubble, but because of a pack of once-domesticated dogs gone feral. The truth of this legend I have yet to establish. However, the feral nature of the foxes inclines me to believe that the animals with whom I share a neighbourhood only need so much desperation to get very bold indeed. Since World War II, property in London has become ever more valuable. The scraps of edge land which once were the domain of urban foxes are disappearing, forcing them out into parks and gardens.

It would seem that Nature, whether four-footed-and-furry or bark-and-leaf, is remarkably ingenious at making comebacks. In the last chapter about abandoned spaces, I dealt briefly with the medicine which those spaces offer us: friendship with the rest of the creatures on this earth, and a drive to address the environmental mistakes our species is so good at making. Below I'll take this theme farther, looking at what practical, spiritual lessons the stubbornness of the nature found in our cities has to teach us.

Defining stubborn nature

Unpopular opinion number two of this chapter: in addition to my great dislike of foxes, I am not a fan of indoor potted plants. Aside from the occasional cactus or maybe a potted tree, I just can't get on board with the 1970s potted plant revival that is en vogue at present. Chalk it up to some truly rainforest-ish living situations I've had to cope with in the past, or my own natural clumsiness for knocking over bowls of soil. Whatever it is, I'm just not here for filling my house with All The Plants.

Whether or not you're a lover of potted plants, if you happen to be still reading, thank you. Some people have the gifts to be dedicated #plantwhisperers, and good on you all! Filling your living space with happy green things has been shown to have all kinds of psychological benefits, in addition to improving air quality — something most city dwellers certainly could use help with. Go forth and plant your space up, I say.

Potted plants aren't actually what I mean by 'stubborn nature'. They're cultivated, curated additions to a space which can bring great delight, and they may be stubborn indeed. In fact they usually need to be stubborn to survive our (read: *my*) absentminded watering patterns. The kind of thing I'm talking about with 'stubborn nature' is not that. I am looking for the scrappier, more irregular, less pin-down-able fragments of nature which surprise us by their tenacity in the so-called concrete jungles we humans create.

Recently a friend of mine allowed me to read a draft of a novel of his which involved a young man cycling out of London by bicycle, completely by way of its system of canals. This system is complex and vast. With a few gaps, the canal-committed traveller could go all the way from London to Birmingham, a distance of over 120 miles. Canals and their towpaths, in London or elsewhere, tend to preserve excellent examples of stubborn nature. Water birds, mosses and nettles. Butterflies, damselflies, and fish. Rare flowers, or even just fairly common ones that don't have a chance to grow in well-mown parks.

Canals and towpaths aren't the only spaces where stubborn nature can flourish. Even the most cement-bound tree in a city pavement can play host to a wealth of healthy insect life; at my church we're currently discussing the possibility of keeping bees on our church roof. There are a thousand and one examples of tenacious flora and fauna hanging on to life in the city, with or without human help. To my mind, there are at least three lessons or spiritual practices which these stubborn bits of nature can help us learn: lessons of research, attention & interpretation, and stubbornness itself.

Research

Research may not strike you as much of a spiritual activity. Part of the development of spiritual practices is, though, as I've written above, a cultivation of curiosity. When it comes to the stubborn nature all around you, this means sitting down and giving yourself time to go down those internet rabbit holes about urban spaces where wildlife can thrive: canals, rivers, nature reserves, city farms, allotments, rooftops, railway arches, and so forth. What spaces are there in your city? Which of them sound most interesting to you, most worth checking out?

There is also the old-school way of doing research: by word of mouth. It's always a good idea to do some of our research by actually speaking with others, for two reasons. The first is so that we don't forget that the internet is not the sum total of all human thought and information in existence, and the second is that loneliness is rife in our cities, so sharing our topics of interest and curiosity is a great way to connect with more of our fellow city-dwellers. You could start by bringing up the fact that you are researching urban wildlife in passing conversations, or by having a look at community noticeboards.

A significant spiritual malaise of our time, loneliness can be addressed by the spiritual practice of researching stubborn nature in two ways. Firstly, as with our discussion of neighbourliness in Chapter 5, it is linked to the practice of connecting with neighbours, taking the risk of friendship in a disconnected age. Secondly, we are challenged to think about how far we are willing to extend the boundaries of our friendship — does that include the non-human world too? One cannot be a friend with a tree or a dog or an amoeba in quite the same way as with a human. Does that mean, however, that the human posture towards all other life cannot be one of friendship? I don't think so. In fact, I think that particularly urban, stubborn nature extends to us a friendship which we'd do well to reciprocate.

In the previous chapter I touched on the important medicine we are offered by visiting abandoned spaces which are being reclaimed by nature. The nature of this medicine is an ethical one: a 'we must' or 'we could' or 'together we can' act with greater solidarity or grace towards the other life on this earth, for the benefit of all life on this earth. However, as the great ethical writers of many traditions have urged, humans don't tend to make good ethical choices only by feeling a sense of 'should', pushed by a sense of guilt for something we've done wrong or neglected to do. Rather more effectively we are pulled towards ethical behaviour (in this case, love for our planet and environmental care) by something good, something holy, something virtuous, a gut instinct, a virtue of *friendship* with the nature that is so stubborn around us.

The role of plant and animal life in guiding humanity towards a deeper spirituality is held in high importance in a variety of religious traditions. Indigenous traditions especially, with their historic connections to specific regions and ecosystems, have preserved this religious impulse in vibrant ways. I particularly love the writing of Kaitlin Curtice of the Powatomi nation, and Richard Twiss of the Sicangu Lakota Oyate, both of whom wrestle in their work with the heritage of global Christianity and their indigenous identities, particularly with regards to attitudes to the land and nature.[7] Within wider Islam, Hinduism and Christianity, a common marker for holy people or saints is that they are close to particular trees or animals, sometimes eschewing human company for that of other creatures. (We can all relate to that impulse after a long day at work, can't we?)

In densely urban contexts, we have to be intentional and persistent about our research into the stubborn nature around us. We have to be willing to let our definition of friendship expand, for our souls' sake. We might find it more of a task to notice the changing of the seasons, and might not automatically feel connected with, or like we are able to befriend, particular plants and animals. These are obstacles, however, which with a bit of effort and — dare I say — stubbornness, we can get past.

---

[7] Part of your research might be into particular spiritual traditions and how they have stayed close to plant and animal life, and whether there is particular wisdom there for those who live in urban areas. Find out about the land you live on and which nations have historically lived there & learn to acknowledge your forebears, both tribal and natural.

Paying attention & interpreting what you see

Once you have gone about finding out about the spaces in your city where stubborn nature might thrive, what does it look like to spend time there? During your research, your curiosity will have had time to brew and strengthen; maybe you'll have noticed some stubborn nature already in your regular routes along the pavement. What next? At this point, I often turn to poetry. The late poet Mary Oliver wrote brilliant, concise and energetic poetry which celebrated the natural world. She had a lot to say about *paying attention* as the work of not only writing but — more universally — spirituality. In 'Sometimes', she writes,

[...]
Instructions for living a life:
Pay attention.
Be astonished.
Tell about it.
[...]

And, just as emphatically, she writes in 'Yes! No!,'

[...]
To pay attention,
this is our endless
and proper work.
[...]

Attention is not only the domain of writers. My favourite scene in the film *Girl with a Pearl Earring* is one in which the master painter, Vermeer, realises that the servant woman Griet can describe the colours in the clouds outside their Amsterdam townhouse as, 'No, not white. Yellow, blue, and grey.' Griet is able to pay attention and see past the surface colour of the clouds to those which make them up their depth.

Thank goodness you don't need to be a poet or a painter to pay attention. When it comes to seeking the stubborn nature around you in the city, and learning its lessons, all you need to do is slow down and spot what's all around you. This is absolutely basic. Unless you are looking up, for example, you're not going to spot where that beehive is starting in the corner of the eaves above the cashpoint at the bank. Unless you take a slightly different route to the bus for work and walk only half your normal speed, you might miss the wild mallow plant blooming next to the front step of that house that's for sale. Awareness of and attentiveness to the present moment is the foundation of all mindfulness-based practices.

Awareness and attention, however, are just the first part. After that comes the slower, more intuitive and effortful practice of learning from what you see. From many years of conversations with friends, colleagues and parishioners about this spiritual practice, I've found that it comes naturally to some and not so much to others. At the core of this practice is a sense of trust in what strikes you about what you see — a trust that these impressions and associations could constitute nudges from the Divine. It is a trust that your own symbolic-interpretive powers have been well-formed by your faith practice or spiritual tradition, so that they are useful not only in formal settings for worship, meditation, prayer or learning, but also in the everyday.

To pay attention is to offer someone or something a sacred *gaze*: the divine look of love, which transforms what it sees because it sees with not only eyes but also heart.

I've spent decades soaking in a spiritual tradition that shapes my interpretive powers and insists on a belief in the heart-voice, the inner voice, having something to do with God, not just my own random thoughts. I trust myself to look slowly at a film scene — or a clump of trees, a stray wild mouse, a pattern in some lichen — and to discern meaning. This faithful act that forms a significant part of my daily spiritual practice and it's one I offer you, not only because it is endlessly creative and generative, but also fun. The dynamism and life in your city means that different insights present themselves each time you encounter aspects of your city and its stubborn nature afresh.

As with any practice of discernment or divination, it is easy to be tempted away from trust: trust in the ability of the Divine to meet you in these snippets of stubborn nature, and in your own ability to apprehend Their presence. The first temptation is basically just reductive cynicism. You go out for your lunch break, walk along a canal which is covered by greenish algae slime, which makes you think of mushy peas and then before you know it you're writing a grocery list in your head. *Wait a minute. That's just a quotidian chain of thoughts. Where is God in all that? Sure it's nice to stop and think for a moment and sure we could always do with a bit more meal planning, but maybe this whole practice is ridiculous, just letting your thoughts wander and pretending God might speak to you somewhere.* I have certainly gone down this cynical line of thinking before, and you probably will, too. When that happens: keep your courage. Remember not to split the world into 'sacred' stuff and 'secular' stuff: it is all one, and God is to be found in it all.

The second temptation is to lose touch with our self trust. You go out for that canal walk, see that green slime, and feel utterly uninspired by it. Who wouldn't? It's slime. But you might begin to think, *What am I doing wrong? How could I ever think that my own interpretations of mundane stuff could be spiritually insightful?* Again: nothing is wrong. You're fine. Maybe the slime isn't your spiritual lesson for the day — it's someone else's, or no one's. Trust yourself stubbornly.

I want to say with certainty that not every moment you spend seeking out, slowly seeing, and making interpretive space for the stubborn nature in your city is going to yield Huge Spiritual Revelations to your life. Wouldn't that be exhausting? Sometimes a crow is just a crow, or an earwig is just an earwig. This practice will be quietly eventful, rarely earth-shattering, and therefore something you can sustain and something which spiritually sustains you.

The virtue in stubbornness

If you hop in a car or a train and get right out of your city for a day, you can have a great time doing some 'slow seeing' surrounded by a natural landscape. You won't have to look for stubborn nature because you'll be immersed in a rural setting. That said, I remain stubbornly committed to the idea that the practice of seeking stubborn nature isn't inferior to 'forest bathing' or any other type of rural retreat, *especially because* it is more difficult for that life to thrive in urban spaces.

I began this book by insisting that a spirituality which requires constant escapism isn't one in which anyone should linger. This doesn't mean that you should never enjoy taking a day or longer outside your city. (I'll deal directly with that theme in the next chapter.) What it does mean is that if you're always looking for a way out, you'll certainly find it hard to learn to pay attention to what is in front of you, to see it slowly and to grow to trust that inner voice which teaches you lessons from what you see.

The tenacity and endurance of the wildlife in your city can teach you to develop your own tenacity and endurance, especially when it comes to the spiritual life. This is where stubbornness can become truly a virtue. This is a stubbornness to grow and thrive, rather than a stubbornness that shuts down compromise, conversation or relationship. Spiritual stubbornness, inspired by the stubborn nature around you in the city, is an insistence on learning, seeing and growing even amidst great obstacles. It's something we all have the choice to pursue, and something about which urban wildlife is an excellent teacher.

Spiritual stubbornness also asks us to question inherited narratives, not only the tempting narrative of escapism but also any narrative that tells us not to trust that our inner voice could be entwined with the voice of the Divine. Certainly there's always a parsing of that voice to be done, paying attention to the life, dynamism, challenge in it, learning what of it is beneficial to us and what's not. That's where the adventure lies.

As we finish with the topic of stubbornness, though, a quick caveat: don't forget how aggressive stubbornness can be sometimes, no matter how much spiritualising we might do of the concept. It's crucial to couple it with some humility. Without humility, stubbornness becomes an end in itself, a self-reinforcing feedback loop which is the opposite of thriving: it becomes destructive.

Sacred Pavement: Finding stubborn nature

The ambiguity in stubbornness brings me back to where I began this chapter: my ongoing struggle with the foxes. Those are some utterly stubborn creatures. Cute and playful and determined, yes, but certainly destructive. Now, as they're foxes I don't expect them to suddenly develop or act out human concepts like humility. That would be taking anthropomorphism a bit too far. Their stubbornness and destructiveness comes with a cost, not just to my garden but also their other urban habitats. Perhaps, some days, the lesson they have for me *is* humility, because of how they live quite riskily without it. This lesson is one I could not learn from them unless, despite my frustration, I had enough humility to acknowledge that there was something to be learned. In a nutshell, that's the practice of finding stubborn nature: finding it (through research), paying attention and intuiting its lessons, including those lessons about stubbornness itself.

Urban Adventures

1. *Research time.* Sketch out a map of your city or a part of it on a double-page spread of your journal, it need not be too detailed. As you go about researching the spaces in your city where urban wildlife can thrive, represent these on this map, so you know where to go looking. You could choose different colours and symbols to represent different types of spaces: get as creative as you like with this.

2. *Botanica Urbanica.* Be a sidewalk naturalist for a few days: create your own mini urban wildlife encyclopedia with the wildlife that you find. Add in mythical creatures linked to the city's lore if you like! Research their actual scientific / Latin names, or make some up.

3. *Inside Out.* Find a walking route that will take you from the centre of your city completely out of it into the countryside. Copy a map of that route into a page spread in your journal, and document the walk. If you are unable to walk long distances, use public transport to stop at key points along the way.

4. *Guerilla gardening.* Is there a stray patch of soil somewhere near you where you could quietly plant something? A seedling is probably hardier than a seed if it's an area with heavy foot traffic. Check in regularly on your plant friend — can they make it past the end of a season?

CHAPTER 9

There and Back Again

'We're sorry, but we haven't managed to get your work visa paperwork together in time. You'll need to return to the USA for a while and wait while we complete your application process.'

These words — hedged in slightly more professional English — hit me like a sledgehammer in the autumn of 2010. I'd been hired by a youth work charity I really liked to do a job I was excited by and qualified for, with a rather miraculous little studio flat available to me in Central London. I was in love with my (English) partner, involved in my local community, thoroughly besotted with the strange wonderful weirdness of being a Londoner. I'd begun to become my adult self, living in this global city on this small island in the North Sea.

Record scratch: the Home Office gave me my marching orders. Clinging tenaciously to the belief that all would sort itself out in time, I packed my life up into my two suitcases and retreated to my parents' house and my childhood bedroom. Within a month my cabin fever was intense, so I took a job in a pizza shop that was never meant to last long. When I did extra delivery shifts in the afternoon, the residents of the county where I'd grown up would look me up and down in confusion, often saying, 'Why are *you* delivering pizzas?' Why, indeed. *How much time have you got?* I wanted to ask. *Your pizza will get cold.*

Three months in and it was early December. Despite weekly calls to London to chase down my would-be employer, no work visa had materialised. The HR department couldn't seem to get their act together, and at last they told me so plainly. No job. My studio flat, empty for three months and costing my landlord money, was given away to another tenant. Two weeks before Christmas, just off the back of all this, my partner and I broke up. Somehow I didn't see it coming.

I am a lover of snow, and snow comes early in rural Michigan. I remember the days after these events hazily: watching the flakes tumble down whilst sitting on my parents' couch cuddling their old basset hound. For the first time the snow brought me no joy. I had taken a couple sick days from the pizza shop — never before had I missed work because of mental health rather than physical. My feelings veered between depression and self-criticism. How on earth did I think that this moving-to-London thing was a good idea? Why did I think I deserved such an outlandish opportunity? After several days of inert sitting, not eating, being caught up in the mire of my thoughts, I decided that I needed to get some fresh air and walked down the long icy driveway to the mailbox. The walk which normally was 10 minutes took me at least half an hour this time, there and back. The wind was cutting and the puddles had frozen over; the sky was enduringly grey but at least the air was fresh. It was so hard to lift my head and look up with no hopeful blue above but I tried to do so, tried to breathe deeply, tried to figure out what I was supposed to do now.

I'd never been a person given to charismatic spiritual experiences or extraordinary clairvoyance, or so I thought then.

But halfway down the driveway, in that way that is impossible to describe, I perceived the voice of One who was not just my inner voice. They said, 'You're more than this.' More than a failed job, a failed move, a failed relationship, dashed hopes. More than a defeated graduate living half on my parents' goodwill, tossing pizzas for seven dollars an hour plus tips, wondering what to do with her life, how she was going to pay her student loan bill when it arrived.

In the years since that day I've discovered the practice of walking labyrinths. On that day, the driveway was all the labyrinth I needed. Much less twisty though equally treacherous, walking it slowly I was able to hear from God in a way that was blessedly more succinct than usual. The encouraging message was brief but I returned to the house feeling a tiny bit more able to move on. It was still ten days to midwinter, bleak as ever. I still had to answer the endless questions from visiting family and friends over Christmas: how's it going? Where are you working? Putting that degree to use? Are you back in the country for good? When are you going to get married, settle down, make your mom a grandma? (Don't you just *love* extended family?) But that walk had been the turning point.

All that long winter, plans were forming, ones that might include me being back in London. Part of me didn't want to jinx them (or deal with potential disappointment publicly) by announcing them too soon. As an extrovert this was driving me batty, so as soon as the worst of the season's blizzards were past and the county ploughs were able to keep up with road cleaning, I decided I'd buy myself some good sneakers and teach myself how to run. I'd always hated running in gyms, not being very fit, but gasping my way down mostly deserted country lanes was acceptable. For ten months, come rain, snow, or shine, I got up, threw on whatever layers the weather demanded, and ran. It started with about a mile loop, which then grew to two, three, or four.

At the end of those ten months, having learnt just as much about physical as about spiritual and emotional endurance, I boarded a plane back to England. I had something like a plan, tenuous though it was and gingerly though I embarked on it. That life had come together in this way for me to go back still felt like a surprise, like something that might disappear at any moment. But it also felt right, like something worth trusting as far as I could.

That was nine years ago, and it wasn't the last time that I thought I was going to be leaving London, my adopted hometown, for good. At times I've longed to leave, an experience which is probably familiar. Reckoning with the pull this city has on me has been a spiritual endeavour which began with that original ordeal back in Michigan, where I heard something of the voice of God and where I took up running to keep me sane and keep me praying. Since then, and through the experience of other, shorter-term travels, I've begun to use what those travels have taught me spiritually and form particular spiritual practices around them. I've begun to expect to be met by that divine voice, even and especially when I'm away from the city I call home.

City gravity

For good and ill, cities have their own pull to them, like small moons with their own gravitational field. To rocket out of them takes energy, whether or not you are going for a short or long time, of your own volition or because you are required to leave. Throughout this book I've urged you to live out your spirituality in cooperation with your urban environment, not in spite of it by only sustaining your inner life with brief escapes. That key point aside, you will have cause to leave from time to time: for work, for family, for holiday. Part of being a city-dweller is coming to terms with this almost tidal experience of going and coming back.

What about, as with my personal story above, the choice about leaving a city is made for you, by job or responsibilities or your immigration status? The lack of choice you might have in situations like this is deeply frustrating, even traumatising. The energy it takes to leave the city is demanded of you on a time scale not often your own, and there aren't any relative assurances of coming back. These sorts of leavings don't feel gentle and the metaphor of tides, gentle leavings and returnings, does not suit. These leavings feel more like exile. We are required to draw on all our spiritual and emotional resources to find new gravity and a new equilibrium wherever we wind up.

Neither the tidal experiences of going and returning nor the times of exile are comfortable states in which to be. But they're part of what it means to be a living, breathing being in this world which is full of change. As the practice of exploring the hidden aspects of our cities brings up shadows, so the practice of going and returning allows us to explore the spiritual aspects of lack, disorientation and exile. Sometimes our hardest-won, least comfortably-learnt spiritual lessons are the ones which truly stick.

Going away: experiencing lack

Let's start on the sunny side, with the experience of voluntarily going and coming back. For my work, a few years back, I traveled to the freezing and fascinating city of Newcastle. It was only for three days and the work wasn't onerous, but it was enough to bring up that odd feeling of missing a place, missing my home. I recognised this feeling from when I'd had to go back to the USA, along with an odd sense of guilt, because it wasn't necessarily people I missed (though there were plenty of those) but my home city itself.

I returned to a question which has been with me for much of my life: what does it mean to miss a place, after all? Can we really do it? Faith traditions around the world certainly seem to think so, conceptualising this longing, this experience of geographical lack, with strong attachments to holy regions or lands, whether these can be visited in pilgrimage or have been lost to the sands of time. What is it, however, that we are longing *for* when we are away from a place? Different sensory experiences are the dressings on the window — perhaps we miss the particular birds that we can hear when we first wake up in the morning, the colours and smells of our neighbourhood, the view that greets us when we turn that one corner.

To my mind, what we really miss is *how we are able to be* in that place. We miss a version of ourselves, one who was able to find our way about with confidence or ease. We miss being caught up in a web of interactions, relationships and patterns. We miss how we were able to connect with the Divine there. All these missings are in the context of relationships — with Spirit, with others, with ourselves — which enrich our experience of a place beyond just observation, sensory appreciation, or objective beauty.

Experiencing the lack of these particular relationships when you go away from a place can be odd, disjointed, or even painful. The easiest relationships to adjust to lack are, perhaps, those we have with other people or living creatures. We can accept more easily that they're not here with us. The lack of them might hurt, but it makes sense. Harder to accept is the sense of lack we feel within our relationship with Spirit, or with ourselves. Why should those relationships change? We've not left ourselves, nor has Spirit suddenly stopped being the ground of all being including our own. So why should we be feeling the lack in those places, too?

When we travel, the patterns that we've developed of relating to ourselves and to the Divine inevitably change — even for the most routine-averse among us! You don't need to be a person who hates change and adheres strictly to a set of daily rituals to sense these shifts. They create in us a sense of lack: missing who we normally are and missing where and how we practice our spirituality.

What I want to emphasise here is that this experience of lack, though it might be uncomfortable, is a good and useful thing. Being forced temporarily out of certain ways of being and behaving is healthy, because it draws our awareness to the habits we've developed intentionally or not so intentionally. Going away from the city where we call home, either to another urban area or somewhere completely different, gives us a foil for our daily life. If we pay attention, we are able to better see and understand what life will be waiting for us when we get back.

There is a spiritual 'nutritious value' to experiencing this lack. Multiple traditions within the umbrella of Buddhism, as well as the ascetic traditions within Protestant and Roman Catholic Christianity, acknowledge the importance of not-having. An experience of lack is not undergone solely to generate gratitude: giving up something for a while so we can appreciate it better when we have it again. On the contrary, such an experience is meant to draw our attention deeper than on our surface possessions and patterns so we can hear what we are really lacking, desiring, or needing beneath all the *stuff*. There's a huge power in the acknowledgement of something we lack, need or desire — even and especially if that thing isn't something we can locate immediately.

For example, say you go away to visit a grandparent who lives a few hours away. You're staying in their house, which throws all your routines off. You miss your friends. You even find yourself beginning to miss things you normally find a bit of a drudgery in your work! Beyond these things, something else is off. It's hard to find time to meditate. You keep running into people who knew a version of you from years ago and want to interact with you as if you were still that person. Despite all these frustrations and the fact that you'd really like to be back in your everyday life, there's something about the gentle space and care shown to you by this grandparent, something about the way they tentatively entrust to you their extraordinary life stories, which makes you realise that you lack a connection with older folk like this in your daily life. This quietly radical, caring and self-assured, rambly and generous presence.

Take another example: a long-awaited, long-saved-for holiday to a place you've always wanted to visit. Again, all the routines are off, even if that's a welcome change involving not setting an alarm most days. The place is somewhere you always longed to travel, somewhere incredibly different to the city where you live. So different, in fact, that you are quite overwhelmed. You brushed up on the local language, but it's tough going. Despite this you're loving the exploration of this place, the major and minor sights. Seeing them you feel not only a sense of curiosity you haven't felt in a long time, but an ability to pray in ways that are hard to squeeze into your daily life. This curiosity and this ease in spiritual practice, how had you not noticed these things were missing in your life?

Coming back home is the easy part, having been jolted out of your routine enough to realise what you lack. Having become attuned to a desire because of a change in scenery, the challenge is how to ask and follow where that desire leads you when the patterns and pressures of daily life resume. As usual, the effort is in asking and answering the question, *What happens now?*

Coming back: experiencing disorientation

One of the major strands of my own spiritual practice is one of chanting the Psalms, a book from the Hebrew Bible incorporated into the Christian scriptures. For the unfamiliar, the Psalms are a set (a 'psalter') of 150 poems that run the gamut of human experience and emotion. I learned about chanting them from monastic communities, many of whom still strive to chant all 150 every week, and also from the writer Cynthia Borgeault, whose work on contemplative prayer I can't recommend highly enough. I don't try to get through all the Psalms in a week, but I can just about manage it in a month if I'm persistent.

Chanting the whole Psalter with this regularity is seen by a lot of people, Christian and otherwise, as a pointless practice — a kind of boring, mindless mumbling, time that could be better spent in silence or in some other form of prayer. Yet for thousands if not millions of people around the globe, it is a crucial practice because of the sheer breadth of experience contained within those poems. Trust, anger, hope, fear, ecstasy, worry, contentment, jealousy, joy... they're all there, and more besides. Part of praying these psalms is about singing into being a picture of the whole constellation of human experience, wherever I feel I might be located in that constellation at the moment. I don't necessarily identify with the words I'm chanting one hundred percent, but sometimes I do. Either way, there is a bigger picture than me, a bigger song in which I take part. My friend Kate likes to point out that especially when we can't identify the psalms we are praying, we pray them in solidarity with others in the world who can and do. Our prayer becomes, as it always has been, about so much more than just ourselves and our feelings.

Most of the psalms, as the scholar Walter Bruggemann points out, follow a cycle: orientation (setting the scene of how things are), disorientation (something happens, usually unforeseen and not always good), and reorientation (making sense of the new world the poet is in, with reference to Divine faithfulness and their own experience). Noticing this cycle is another reason why psalm-singing is important to many. The psalms capture in sacred microcosm the many hurdles and challenges of the spiritual life.

Coming back home to the city after the disruption of travel is an experience of reorientation. Something has happened, leaving and coming back, experiencing lack in multiple ways. To come back afterwards is to move from the disorientation into reorientation. What did your travel show you about your normal life that you think might need to adjust? This can be as simple as a holiday giving you space to rest, and you realise you want to make more time to rest in your average week, or it could be something deeper or more active. Only the disorienting experience of going and coming back can help you listen out for the lack. The reorientation process is yours to engage in as much as you will.

Allowing myself space for this reorientation has become a key part of my own travel — lest I lose the valuable insights which came up for me while I was away. There's nothing wrong with just having a pleasant, restful holiday and acquiring some lasting memories. That said, I find that if I don't make space for reorientation, even these loveliest of memories feel unintegrated into the rest of my life. I find myself with a lingering sense of lack of continuity between the person I was there and the person I am here.

Reorientation is, for me, about having a day between the travel and getting back into normal life if at all possible. Obviously it's a day to do practical things like laundry, sleeping off jet lag, putting the suitcase away and sorting out the snail mail, but it's also about just letting my body and soul settle back in. I take some time to ruminate on what my going-away has brought up for me spiritually: what I've realised I want or need in my normal life that I just don't have, and how I might let that shape my plans going forward. I also try to give myself a bit of a break for the first few days back in everyday life. I just assume that I'm going to be less productive and more distractible. That first post-holiday run is going to be a tough one, and that's fine. Whatever a practice of reorientation might look like for you — it's primarily about a bit of extra space, and extra grace towards yourself and others. There'll be more below in the Urban Adventures about how you might experiment and find your own practices in this vein.

Exile: strangers in a strange land

Often when I speak to native Brits about their travels in America, I am told some form of a joke which goes like this. 'Yes, we liked New York, loved Disneyland and didn't understand Las Vegas. It was a great holiday except for the language barrier.' I always laugh, because my momma taught me to be polite; I know a truly British response would be to make some disparaging remark about Americans and then an even harsher jibe at my interlocutor. But I've never quite mastered this form of banter.

The playwright George Bernard Shaw supposedly originated the saying that Britain and America are 'two countries divided by a common language.' The oddness of having chosen my exile, chosen a home amongst those who (sort of) share my language has at different points amused, frustrated and flummoxed me. Living in today's world, with migration on a global scale never far from public view or debate, I'm always aware that my difficulties with immigration systems are minimal compared to what many undergo.

True exile, as I wrote above, is when the choice to leave a place is made for us. When borders are no longer ours to cross freely, when the choice of where to make our homes is not limitless. Themes of exile and return loom large in the Hebrew Scriptures, giving great depth and shape to Jewish concepts and religious practices around land, community and identity. The idea of being a community, even a faith group, in diaspora has emerged from these holy texts and the experiences of Jewish people over the centuries.

The word diaspora is borrowed from Greek, combining *dia-*, a preposition meaning through or across, and *spora(e)*, meaning seeds. To be a community in diaspora, then, is to be a community scattered like seeds to the four winds. In recent years, not only Jewish people but also people of African origin have claimed the word for their social and religious experiences, describing what it means to have been scattered about by several hundred years of the transatlantic slave trade. The fundamental spiritual question amongst diaspora communities is: whither have those seeds fallen and taken root, and what fruit are they now growing?

Not all of us will necessarily identify as being part of a diaspora community. What do global experiences of exile and diaspora mean for us then, those of us living in the twenty-first century who are just used to globalisation and the privileges of easy travel? Mostly, I think it is an invitation to us to keep humble and keep learning. Maybe you don't have Jewish or African background, or come from another people group who have experienced exile. What an opportunity, then, to learn deeply from those who have: to read, speak with, and sit at the feet of those whose experiences of exile and diaspora have shaped their individual, communal and spiritual lives.

And what better place to do this learning, this re-imagining of our lives in light of these experiences, than in our cities? The reality of exile and diaspora in our world is also a reminder of the great potential of urban environments to be places where people from all over the world can come to make new lives. There's a reason beyond the ready availability of entry-level jobs that refugee and asylum-seeker resettlement programs take place in urban areas. It is that it's much easier to form new communities here, cheek by jowl.

A colleague of mine once criticised the idea that any city could be a true 'melting pot' of immigrants. This phrase, she said, seemed completely to erase the sense of cultural identities which people bring with them and which, yes, may shift and meld over time. She suggested that a less catchy but truer metaphor was the city as a chef's salad. A mix of distinct parts mostly retaining their individual flavours, but taken together as a unique combination, with the 'dressing' of city life influencing all the composite parts but not drowning them out. I find that the longer I live in urban areas, the more I agree with this picture. This integration-resistant diversity is part of our cities' pull, beauty and spiritual richness. Cultural and spiritual identities don't simply meld into one, a melted combination of all the crayons in the crayon-box into a brownish-greyish goop. They retain some of their particularity in truly inventive ways, some necessitated by the hardship of life in diaspora. This is what makes living in a city of diasporas, of immigrants and exiles, a place of great potential spiritual nourishment, far from the desert some of the countryphiles would have us believe it to be.

Sacred Pavement: There and back again

The purpose of this book is to challenge the narrative of escaping the city which can be so prevalent in faith and spiritual communities. Nevertheless, most of us are likely to leave and come back from time to time. In this chapter I've been careful to reframe this as something other than escape. I've redrawn some of the lines around what it means to go away and come back; it's up to you to colour within these lines or, as is usually a bit more fun, to ignore them, colour around them, and draw in some of your own. You'll find suggestions for all this in the Urban Adventures below.

Touching on the topics of exile and diaspora, however, brings into sharp relief the fact that our ability to control our lives, though great, is always limited — even regarding where we live our lives. I suggest that for those of us who have not experienced exile and who aren't members of diaspora community, we might simply find opportunities to learn from others who have.

Cultivating a learner's mind is key to any spiritual path, no matter how practiced or prayerful we might become. What can we learn from those who have experienced exile? What can it teach us about our relationship to our own longing, our own past, our own ancestors? How can the wisdom gained in exile lead us into greater solidarity with our neighbours, especially those who've been displaced? Asking these questions honestly will bring us to that place where the realms of spirituality and culture, even spirituality and politics, meet. As in so many aspects of our urban spiritual life, this area is one where the spiritual rubber really meets the road.

In the next and final chapter, I'll tackle that other kind of city-leaving, the kind that isn't easily accompanied by return, the kind that requires a good and care-filled farewell. Before we get there, here are your Urban Adventures.

Urban Adventures

1. *Planning around travel: going and coming back.* The next time you are away from your city, pay attention to those deeper things which come up around what you miss or lack, both as a traveller and in your day to day life. Take time every day you are travelling to ask yourself this question and journal about it. Is what you miss what you expected to miss, or something else entirely?

2. *The most obvious mapping.* Use a page or a page spread in your journal to sketch out a map of your travels. You could go macro — drawing continents and how you traverse them — and/or

micro — drawing the immediate area where you are staying. If your map were a map of a pilgrimage, what would be the sacred sites? How would you depict those fellow travellers you met along the way and how they left a mark on you?

3. *Urban travels.* Are you going away from your city to another? The adventures of other sections in this book could apply to cities that aren't your usual home as well. Pick some of the adventures which you've enjoyed the most and practice them in the place you are in temporarily — including the journaling, drawing, meditation, and whatever else you found helpful.

4. *Reorientation.* The next time you are away for work or holiday, build in a full 'reorientation day' at the end of that time. Use it to do your laundry and also to pick up the threads of disorientation that came up while you were away.

5. *Encountering exile.* Make some opportunities to meet people who have been exiled literally and recently: refugees or asylum seekers. Charities which support migrants often welcome even temporary volunteers, and you might be surprised to find people in your local area who have come from further away than you think. Get curious and ask if they will share something of their experiences with you - but keep in mind their story is their own, is probably painful, and they can choose what they tell you. Ask them how their faith or spirituality has been present (or not) throughout. If they're willing, ask if they'll help you draw a map of their journey or journeys in your journal.

CHAPTER 10

Taking your leave

'I hate endings.'

'I don't do goodbyes. I prefer to think of them as "See you laters."'

'Let's say our goodbyes now, so at the airport tomorrow I can keep it together.'

In the past year, each of these have been said to me by different people. Some were new acquaintances who I was unlikely to meet again. Some were friends or neighbours moving out of London for good. Some were colleagues from other countries, people I'll probably not get to work with closely for a long time, if ever. When these kinds of things get voiced at the end of a visit, a conference call, or a house move, I must admit I'm usually left at a loss. Why?

Secretly, I love making an end. Does that make me seem like a heartless person? What I mean isn't that I love living far from dear friends and family or enjoy standing at an airport security desk watching someone walk off with a piece of my heart in their suitcase. That stuff sucks. It hurts. I feel pain and sadness when the thump of the moving van door announces that another one of my dear neighbours will from now on be a long train ride, instead of a bike ride, away. Somewhere, however, underneath all this melancholy, the finality of making an end and marking it well fills me with a sense of relief. Again, not relief that one of us is going. Rather I feel a strange sense of fullness, of completion, that whatever chapter we've been in is now closed. The more meaningful an end that can be made of that closing-of-the-chapter, the better. This is why I am never quite sure how to answer someone who tells me they hate endings, who would rather avoid marking them in any significant or public way.

The peace I've made with endings has come, a little bleakly perhaps, from the fact that helping people mark endings is part of my work. I take funerals, usually one or two a month but sometimes more. Often I get asked the question, 'What's the worst part of your job, is it funerals?' It is always interesting to answer truthfully that no, I find funerals to be one of the most fulfilling parts of my ministry, and to see how people react to this answer. Funerals, though they're usually sad, are immensely important events, marking a person's passing from the known into the unknown. They're about the person who has died as much as they are about the mourners. Striking the balance between the needs of the former and the latter can be tricky at times. Ultimately I trust in the truth, rhythm and symbolic power of the ritual in which I lead people: a ritual of making a farewell.

This isn't a book chiefly about funerals, death or pastoral ministry, but I bring up my experience as a funeral officiant because I think that a lot of us dread endings, and that has something to do with how we've encountered endings in our lives, often in the context of funerals. Most of us will, at some point, move away from the city which we've called home for a time. This is an ending, just as much as is moving across town, changing jobs, or bidding farewell to a person. Such endings deserve as much care as does planning a good sendoff for a departed loved one. Without this care and intention woven into our endings, we run the risk of only valuing our present reality once it has gone. Bidding farewell to the what, the whom, and the where is painful, but crucial.

Whether you are leaving a long-time home, or simply a city that has had a profound impact on you in a relatively brief time, the way in which you take your leave is a deeply spiritual act. I've spent relatively little time in the cities of Rochester, New York; Marrakech; Washington, D.C., and Reykjavík, but they've all shaped me somehow — and in large part, I believe, because I bothered to bid them farewell deliberately. In this chapter, nearly our last one together, I want to spend some time thinking on what will make for a good urban ending.

You don't know what you've got 'til it's gone

We're not great at valuing what we have until it's taken from us — at least, I know I'm not. Recently, a brilliant pub around the corner from me closed. It had one of the best pub names ever — The Water Poet — and a lovely, rambly interior which gave way to a garden where old chesterfield sofas beckoned. I'd had many an awkward first date there in the wintry glow of the heat lamps, escaping whatever soccer match was on the indoor screens. When it was announced that the pub was closing, the outcry in the neighbourhood was well-deserved; the closing was more about ridiculous rent hikes and soulless corporate developments than a natural ending or retirement of the owners.

But when I found myself signing a petition to keep it open, I couldn't help but feeling a little dishonest. I hadn't been to the pub in at least two or three years. It was no longer 'my local'. As much as I'm generally against unethical rent and thoughtless development, I couldn't *really* say to myself that I'd valued or supported the pub recently. I hadn't known how much I valued it until it was almost gone.

Partially because of this tendency to forget to value what we have while we have it, we aren't great at marking endings. We do well at marking beginnings with rituals, celebrations, or tokens... but endings not so much. Aside from funerals themselves, where can we find a healthy appreciation of endings, and what rituals do we have in our communities for making an end? Going out for a drink with colleagues before you leave a job is one. Can you think of many others?

Rituals for dealing with the grief of any ending don't seem to be something at which western cultures excel, at least not in the current era. We experience the grief of endings; we might cry, might seek people with whom to process this grief, but that's often as far as it goes. Grief isn't comfortable and it can be embarrassing, but is that any reason for it not to be honoured? On the contrary, the capacity that we have to deal with our uncomfortable, unsightly experiences is just as much a measure of our spiritual depth as is our capacity for dealing with that which is enjoyable or easy to share.

When it comes to saying goodbye to a city where we have spent some time, I think there are two major themes, or archetypes, which are helpful, and which religious traditions have shaped and been shaped by. They are the archetype of death itself, as

I've mentioned, and the archetype of the sojourner. I'll take each of these in turn.

DEATH SPEAKS IN CAPITAL LETTERS

The late Terry Pratchett, an author of considerable humour, wit and warmth, created a hooded, Grim-Reaper-esque character of DEATH who pops into his novels frequently. Rather than being a horror, however, Death has the ultimate dry wit. He (or she?) goes around delivering blunt and mundane messages in a monotone-but-not-shouty ALL CAPS, rather like a goth teenager all grown up. I've always thought that this character was a little stroke of genius in how it draws on the Death archetype. Pratchett doesn't minimise Death's presence — Death shows up when the plot is going to contain some death — but Pratchett also gives Death some suitably black humour. Death gets into petty arguments, expresses annoyance, and is altogether more of a personality than one might expect.

Pratchett's version of Death is spooky but also befriendable. It is this befriending of Death as an archetype of endings which I think a lot of global Westerners are missing out on these days. Creating rituals around endings can help us to do this befriending. I do think that those of us in the west are rediscovering some of these rituals, or at least curiosity around death. Death Cafés, an initiative to get people speaking openly and without agenda around issues of death and dying, continue to grow in popularity. You can train to be a 'death doula' or midwife. Courses and discussion days around all the issues around what makes a good death are offered by clinics, community centres, and religious organisations alike. In Catholic devotion at least two images of sacred death have made it down through the centuries: through the Mexican folk tradition of Santa Muerte (Saint/Holy Death) and through the Franciscan Canticle of the Sun with its fond image of Sister Bodily Death.

Activities, images and pathways around death are proliferating. To me, this reflects a wider longing for more older and deeper ways of being and connecting with death as a final reality — making our peace with our own and others' deaths. The ancient practice of *memento mori*, keeping one's death in mind, included the wearing of small symbols of bone to help people remember to live well, having prepared to die well.

But what about death not just in the literal sense, but as an image of endings more generally? Death can symbolise drastic change and transformation. It can symbolise the end of a time in an urban environment which has shaped us. In Chapter 5, I mentioned the reality of missed opportunities being part of the urban experience of neighbourliness. In our fast-paced cities, we simply can't connect meaningfully with all the people we'd like to. One of the things we'll be grieving when we leave a city, are these myriad missed opportunities to meet and be met by all the vibrant lives alongside whom we have lived. This kind of retrospective, relational fear-of-missing-out is part of the grieving process: part of what needs acknowledging when we are getting ready to make an end and move away. This will probably be felt more keenly by the extroverts among us, but it isn't just the people who we'll have missed out on, but places as well. In Chapter 9, I spent a while musing about what it means to miss a place: to miss who you were in that place and how you met with the Divine there.

Whether it's people, places, opportunities, or a combination of all three which we know we'll miss when we leave, the grief of leaving strikes in unpredictable ways. In Max Porter's *Grief is the Thing with Feathers,* Porter imagines grief as a crow: a snarky trickster, present, unpredictable, an ultimate and unlikely caretaker. (He stops shy of making Grief speak in ALL CAPS.) Grief doesn't play by the rules: it doesn't always wait until after an ending to swoop in. Many people experience the grief of leaving in the lead up to the event itself. Like real death and the real grief which accompanies it, the grief which accompanies leaving our urban homes is something which cannot be controlled any more than we would try and catch a crow. We can simply make space for it to arrive and to stay as long as it wants.

If you've lived in a city for a long time, the city will have been changing around you constantly. You'll have had to endure dozens of smaller endings and transformations: the moving away of loved ones, the closing of that cafe you loved, the fizzling out of a group of friends, the bulldozing of your old place of work. Suddenly when the change is your moving out of town — something you initiate, not just endure — it is possible to feel lost in the grief of it, as if you really are being bereaved. This is because you've moved from passive endurance of change to active making of change, which can be pretty exhausting and confusing. Other factors may have brought on the change and you may not feel it has been 100% your choice: but in the end you are the one giving your landlord notice, planning phone calls and visits with your friends, and asking the corner shop for their extra cardboard boxes so you can pack up your stuff. Intense grief or no, this is a death which you can see coming. At these times it is more important than ever to look this death in the eye, meeting them as you choose to move towards them, and perceive that they are more sacred than scary.

Sojourn awhile

Death itself is one archetype of change, Sojourning is another. Sadly, 'sojourn' is a lovely word which isn't used widely today. If you've heard it at all, you're probably either a lover of Romantic poetry (it shows up a fair bit in Keats, for example) or interested in the history of racial justice in the USA. During the 19th century in the American South, Sojourner Truth lived a remarkable life. She escaped slavery, sued her former owner for the rights to her own son and became a speaker and campaigner for the women's and anti-slavery movements. Born Isabella Bohmfree, she gave herself the name Sojourner Truth because she felt she had a divine calling to speak and 'share the hope that was within her'. This idea of a divine calling to share one's inner hope is lifted directly from the pages of Christian scripture, as is the idea of being a sojourner, meaning one who stays somewhere temporarily, or more spiritually speaking, one who is always being called onward.

The emergence of the music of 'spirituals' during the era of widespread enslavement of Black people in the USA relied heavily on the concept of sojourning, which may have been where Sojourner Truth first encountered the idea. Spirituals — which W. E. B. DuBois also called *sorrow songs* — are songs full of religious hope, lament, and longing for freedom, in this life and in the next. Drawing heavily on biblical language of crossing rivers, ascending to other realms, and being set free as in the Hebrew Exodus of old, these spirituals were able to manifest hopefulness because they held only lightly to the pain of the present; acknowledging it and lamenting it, yes, but not letting it have the last word. Being a sojourner in this life meant raging and working against pain and injustice, but also being aware of one's citizenship, one's belonging, in a world beyond the present one.

Certainly, Christianity is not the only belief system to have space for this kind of wider belonging or conceptualisation of some kind of afterlife. In recent years, beliefs about the afterlife have been frequently oversimplified, almost to the point of caricature. It's not uncommon to encounter the 'pie in the sky' concept of what comes next after this life, with twee assurances on greeting cards aplenty that departed loved ones have somehow become angels sitting on fluffy white clouds. It's enough to make me despair, really. My faith has a much more robust and nuanced hopes in life after death, resurrection and the heavenly realms than this cartoon picture! It's not just Christianity which gets this treatment, of course: other caricatures of religious beliefs around reincarnation or past lives abound in pop culture, too. But I digress.

Whatever your understanding of *what comes next*, the notion of being a sojourner in this life is available to you, to live into as you so choose. To me, it's been a helpful identity or archetype to explore, especially when confronting the grief of leaving places. If I am a sojourner in this life whose 'homeland is heaven' as the

Jerusalem Bible charmingly puts it, then I can expect all other homes and homelands to be temporary. This is as much a challenge as it is a comfort, but then again, so is most spiritual teaching of substance. So are most of the most worthwhile archetypes.

Saying goodbye to a city where you've spent some meaningful days, weeks or years as a sojourner is an altogether more grateful and generous state of soul than saying goodbye, believing you are entitled to stay, or that this change must be wholly bad. As a sojourner, experiencing an ending soul-first is a vulnerable and endlessly valuable rite of passage. Sojourner Truth certainly derived huge strength and energy from living with her eyes fixed beyond the temporal endings, setbacks, and very real suffering of her fellow women and Black kindred. Being a sojourner was her quite literal truth. Might it be yours as well?

Sacred Pavement: Taking your leave

Does anyone much use the phase 'take your leave' anymore? It brings to mind an image of a Victorian gentleman going off in a huff, slamming the door, having been rebuffed by the object of his affection. Given that none of us are Victorian gentlemen, perhaps we can repurpose the word to mean something different, something about how to end a chapter of our lives soulfully? If our departures from cities were done slowly, with intention, by taking time to take our leave, I believe they'd be fundamentally different experiences.

Once, in a discussion about finding time for meditation and prayer with a mentor of mine, this mentor said animatedly to me, 'You can't *make* time for these things. There's only so much time. You have to *take* time from other things.' I didn't like the sound of this, as even to my 21-year-old ears it seemed to smack of anxiety. Of scarcity. Although I'd still want to critique any mindset which relies on scarcity to function, I do think there is some wisdom in what my former mentor said. Namely, that without identifying and following a purpose with our time, it will slip through our fingers like an ever-rolling stream, as the old hymn says. Without taking our time, we lose it. To take our leave is to be purposeful about making an ending somewhere.

For those of you who find the language of 'taking' too aggressive, consider: in contemporary English, we have the words *take* and *receive*. These words have very different connotations. You might feel more accustomed to receiving the experiences which life brings to you, rather than taking them like some sort of exercise in conquest. These words, however, have the same root. In Latin and earlier forms of English and French, one gives rise to the other; in ancient Greek they are one verb. One is incomplete without the other.

To take leave of a city is first to look at what your life has been there. It is taking time (or receiving the gift of time, if you prefer) to see and recognise who you have been in that place, and where God has shown up for you. It involves a willingness to be surprised by the holy coincidences you can spot when you look back, along with the things you perhaps wished had been otherwise. It is giving yourself a chance to realise — in the way that you can only in departure — that the pavement you'd walked on all that time was sacred, no matter how much or how little you made of its sacredness.

After looking back, taking leave is moving forward: allowing yourself to make use of, to live into, the archetypes of death and sojourning, in your spiritual practices and your conversations as you prepare to move. It is treating the whole transition as an urban adventure, whether you're going to another city or to a more rural area, whether you're sad to be leaving or really rather relieved. Put simply, leave-taking is making a good and soulful ending to your time in this urban location.

Leave-taking brings us back to where this book began: on the insistence that Spirit was never to be found in a harried escape from the city but by living more deeply within it. The fathomless well of the Spirit — which is yours to draw from — is not accessible only when you are alone amongst green hills, dramatic deserts, vast seas and plains. It is to be found in any city, maybe even more so, because it requires more of us to find. 'Any idiot,' wrote Lillian Daniel, 'can find God on a mountaintop. The real challenge is finding God in the company of others [especially] those annoying as me.'

With that, dear folks, I'll take my leave.

Urban Adventures

1. *Practicing good grief.* Have a funeral for a place you've left, recently or long ago. Invite a friend or two you can trust. Get some old photos from that time, play a piece of music or have some readings that will remind you of that place. Pray for those you knew well there, for the complexities of that place. What version of yourself were you there? Have you said goodbye to that version of yourself? Make an order of service for this to include in your journal.

2. *What if?* Imagine you did have to leave your city next week for good. What places, people, sounds, or things would you want to say goodbye to? What would you want to say about them, or to them? Can you spend some time with some of these people or things in the coming days, saying what you'd normally wait until the end to say? In the coming days, add a memento, a sketch or a journal entry about these experiences to your journal.

3. *Memento mori.* The tradition of 'keeping your death before you' need not only be literal. It can just mean keeping mementos of significant changes in your past, or an anticipation of those yet to come. What tattoos, jewellery, or precious photos do you have which remind you of closed chapters of your life? Is there a shelf, altar or other space for prayer in your home where you keep them as part of your spiritual practice? Find a way to incorporate these into your journal, either by sketching or tracing them and explaining why they are important.

4. *Sojourning.* Where are the places you have had to leave before, whether urban or rural? Can you represent them together on a regional, national or global map? Draw in the places, the travel and transport between them, the dates, the sojourners themselves.

AFTERWORD

Sorry — I know I said I was taking my leave of you. But I'm popping back in just in case you, like me, love a sneaky second coda. I promised earlier that I'd add some ideas here about how you might use this book together with others. Although a fair bit of the book is meant to be done alone (it's written by an extrovert who knows the struggle of not relying on others to do her spiritual work!) it's definitely worth sharing the path with others. In fact, it may be especially fruitful to share this work with people who are of different faith traditions, spiritual paths, and stages of life to you, not just those who are like-minded. Below are just a few suggestions of ways you might share the pavement.

The book group method

Read the book and discuss it together before heading off on your Urban Adventures. Pizza and rosé not required.

Checking in on the Urban Adventures

Gather a group of friends who want to read and do the Urban Adventures separately, but check in with each other later. Give each other a set period of time in which to do them and then have a discussion group.
- Which of these adventures has led to a practice you might want to keep doing as part of your regular spiritual practice?

- Which was fine that once, but you won't do it again?
- Did anything surprise you as you went about these adventures? Did you find yourself getting really into some of them or avoiding others?

Using this book with the children in your life

Maybe you're a parent, a godparent, or you have some other amazing children in your life. Children's perspectives on spirituality are pure gold, often more profound than many adults'. Do we trust them to share those perspectives with us? Most of the adventures in this book are easily adaptable to include younger people, messier crafty activities, more (or less) noise and more (or less) time that younger people can give to them.

Inside out

Books on spirituality can be notoriously inward-looking or navel-gazing. If you've read this book you know that's not quite how I roll! To be honest, it's not how a healthy spirituality works, either, by separating our inner life and our outer.

One way of using this book 'with others' then might be to share your progress on it with an already existing group or context in your life. Your family, your work colleagues, your spiritual community, your hobby-mates...the list goes on. Rather than expecting them to do all the work with you, you might simply take them along for the ride as you share some of your experiences in conversation.

How could making your way through this book lead to you making a difference in those spheres, either through being of service, changing your point of view, or stepping up to lead in a different way than you could have previously imagined?

Over to you

I'd love to hear from you about whether or not you found it helpful to do this work together, using these suggestions or ideas of your own. You can find me on Instagram at @erinovitch and on Twitter at @e_m_clark.

ACKNOWLEDGEMENTS

So many thanks are due once a book is written. I can't begin to list all the people I'm grateful to here, and will keep the list short.

To George, for his encouragement, mentorship, and ready smile, and all the luminous people at That Guy's House — thank you for hearing me and amplifying my words. For those who gave their encouragements, edits, recommendations and helpful corrections — Joanne, John-Francis, Vanessa, Laura L, Meredith, Laura B, Deena and Kevin.

To the people of St Matthew's Bethnal Green — thank you for putting up with yet another scribbling rector.

To Chloe, for always believing I could. To Kate, for being the first one who rejoiced at the reality of this book with me, and to all those who encouraged me to take on writing a book at the same time as becoming a parish priest as if that weren't more than a little bonkers — thank you for your friendship.

To my brother Ryan, whose always-philosophical conversations helped deepen many of the thoughts and practices in this book.

To Max, who waited for me to learn German whilst I wrote this book, in the words of Gustav Klimt to Emilie Flöge: *Du bist meine Antilope, mein Schatz. Du bist weicher als das Wasser des Himmels.*

ABOUT THE AUTHOR

Erin Clark is an American writer and priest who lives in east London, UK, where she is currently the Rector of St Matthew's Bethnal Green. She has written poetry, fiction and nonfiction in publications such as *Geez, Pilcrow & Dagger,* and *Mash,* and she had a chapter in *The Book of Queer Prophets: 24 Writers on Sexuality and Religion.* Her academic work in theology and sociology concerns the wisdom literature, feminist theologies of embodiment, and shared religious experience beyond confessional boundaries.

When not writing or vicar-ing she can be found wild swimming, walking up hills (urban or rural), or learning to sing bits of plainsong or sacred harp music. She has never quite taken to gardening or remembering to carry an umbrella, despite what people said would happen when she moved to England.

Erin can be found online on Twitter @e_m_clark, and on Instagram @erinovitch.